Narrow Gauge Adventure

The story of the Craig & Mertonford

To my mother, with many thanks for
having patiently endured, for so many years,
my particular form of madness

Published by
Peco Publications & Publicity Ltd.
Beer, Seaton, Devon, EX12 3NA.

ISBN 900586 54 0

Printed by
Sidmouth Printing Works Ltd.,
6-8 Temple Street, Sidmouth, Devon, England
Set in 10 on 12 point Plantin.

P. D. Hancock

Narrow Gauge Adventure

The story of the Craig & Mertonford

and its associated standard gauge lines

A PECO Publication

Foreword

This is a very personal book. It is not a book about how to build a model railway, but is simply an account of one particular model railway layout—and not a very large layout at that. The Craig and Mertonford Light Railway is housed in a room only 12 ft by 10 ft (3.5 by 3 metres). It is built to the popular scale of 4 mm to the foot (approximately 1/76 scale), and it has taken some twenty-five years for it to reach its present state of development. During this time it has been the subject of quite a number of articles in the monthly magazine, "The Railway Modeller", and a certain amount of the material for this book has come from these articles. However, much has had to be rewritten, and much of the story is here told for the first time. The story is not complete, of course, because the model railway itself is not complete, and probably never will be. There is always a host of jobs waiting to be done, there are always new ideas to be incorporated into the general scheme of things, and there will no doubt be at least one more occasion when the whole layout will have to be dismantled and reassembled. It could well be that in another twenty-five years Craigshire will have changed out of all recognition, and then it will be time to sit down and begin writing a second volume to this work.

There is something indefinable about the narrow-gauge atmosphere, and the strange thing is that not all the prototype narrow-gauge lines have it. I personally feel, for example, that some of the African and New Zealand narrow-gauge lines are really "full-size" railways which just happen to run on a narrower than usual track gauge. For me a true narrow-gauge railway has to partake of some of the qualities of the Welsh two-foot gauge lines, or of the Lynton and Barnstaple Railway, or, on a larger scale, of the Isle of Man Railway. I know

vaguely what I am looking for but do not always find it easy to recapture it in model form. I like to think that this photograph of "Alistair" crossing Glenmuir viaduct has managed to capture something of these elusive narrow-gauge characteristics. There is, perhaps, a little bit more of the influence of the American West in this scene than there ought to be, but quite a few British lines did have a sort of "Wild West" atmosphere about them, even to the extent of using American locomotives—so why should the C.M.R. make any apologies?

"Alistair", in fresh green paint and fully lined out, hauls a train of empty hopper wagons over the points into Craig station. The very massive Trix street lamp strikes a somewhat jarring note. Several of these were used as posts for the original tramway overhead but were soon removed.

In between the loading gauge and the lineside hut in the right foreground there is a small puddle of dirty water which never drains away properly and is much appreciated by the local sparrows. In actuality this was just a small piece of broken glass embedded in the pieces of scrap cork which were used to level up the ground between the C.C.W. cork bases upon which the track was laid. The glass was slightly raised from the actual ground, which was painted a mottled green, and the edges of the puddle so formed were planted with weeds consisting of small pieces of sea moss and scraps of loofah.

Contents

1 The idea is born

The person really responsible for Craigshire and the Craig and Mertonford Light Railway is the late John H. Ahern. It was his articles in the wartime and immediate post-war issues of the old "Model Railway News" which fired my schoolboy imagination and led me to take my first tentative steps into the world of railway modelling.

John Ahern's model railway was begun just before the War, and was one of the first successful attempts to model not just a railway, but a railway within a landscape setting. Most of the layouts which were described in the pages of the pre-war model railway magazines were railway and nothing but railway. Models of station buildings, goods sheds, signal boxes and other features of the railway scene were included, of course, but there was usually little attempt at anything save the most perfunctory of lineside scenery.

The perfectly valid argument for this approach was that the modeller was interested primarily in railways and the modelling of railways and that everything else was beyond his "field of reference." An encouragement to this point of view was the fact that, in the larger scales then generally in use, most people simply had very little room to model anything else except the main railway features.

It was the coming of "HO" and "OO" gauge modelling in the late thirties which altered this picture, especially after E. W. Twining and the Rev. Edward Beal had shown just what could be done with the small scales. Edward Beal's articles in the model railway press were full of informative and thought-provoking ideas, and the book which he wrote in 1937 entitled, "The Craft of Modelling Railways" is still a most useful source of reference to anyone fortunate enough to possess a copy.

"Alistair" and train on Glenmuir viaduct. Glenmuir was a very undeveloped "terminus" for the C.M.R., but it did have a certain character. The fact that it was built to sit on top of a pair of bookcases meant that it was about ten inches lower than the rest of the layout, and this gave the opportunity for the viaduct, a waterfall, and a flight of swans. The swans were made from plastic wood with paper wings, and they were attached to the side of the viaduct with thin springy wire which really was fairly invisible unless one knew where to look. Anyway, I liked to think that the illusion of swans flying past the viaduct had been reasonably well achieved.

Edward Beal's own layout was the "OO" gauge "West Midland Railway." This large and complex layout was an inspiration to all who saw or read about it, but, in some ways, its very impressiveness could be a discouragement to a young modeller with very little money and little space available in which to build the model of his dreams. This was where John H. Ahern stepped into the picture. He showed not only that one did not have to have an enormous room for a model railway, but also that there could be just as much fascination in the simplicity of the branch-line railway as in the complexity of the main-line. His own "Madder Valley Railway" (now preserved for us at the Pendon Museum*) was a very simple point-to-point layout which meandered from Madderport, through Much Madder, to Gammon Magna. Madderport was not just the terminus of a model railway—it was a place in its own right, with a harbour, a canal, several streets, and a multiplicity of buildings, all full of charm and character.

I myself first became aware of the Madder Valley and the railway modelling scene in general in 1947 when a friend at school lent me a collection of back numbers of the "Model Railway News." These were more than sufficient to get me started. It was not just the idea of a model railway as such which appealed to me—it was John Ahern's much wider idea of the railway within the landscape. In fact, in my case, I think the modelling possibilities had priority over the railway interest. I wanted to "paint a picture in three dimensions", and, aided by magazines and books from the Public Library, I set to work with a will designing numerous layouts on numerous sheets of cartridge paper. They were not particularly good layouts, and they were all rather academic exercises anyway since at that time my parents and I were living in furnished "digs" and I had no space at all in which to build a layout.

That, of course, did not deter me in the least. Some day, I reasoned, I would have a fine large space at my disposal, and when that day came I wanted to be ready for it. I therefore set to work and designed

* Roye England's venture at Long Wittenham in Berkshire which houses not only the "Madder Valley" but also the meticulously modelled "Pendon Museum of Miniature Landscape and Transport."

a most marvellous layout. It was a scenic layout, of course, but it was also about 30 ft by 20 ft (9 by 6 metres) and it had everything—double main line tracks, flyovers, flyunders, double slip, humpyard, lay-byes and half a dozen stations. We then moved to a house of our own—an Edinburgh tenement flat to be precise—and I came down to earth with a bump. There was no space 30 ft by 20 ft. There was no attic, no basement, no spare room—in fact, nowhere at all for a model railway—unless, that is, I could somehow persuade the household authorities that I needed only half a bedroom to sleep in, and that the other half could very profitably be employed housing a model railway!

I am not quite sure what arguments I used, but, somehow or other, I secured the necessary permission, and before anybody could change their minds I had installed a baseboard consisting of two old blackout frames supported upon a miscellaneous collection of tea chests and packing cases. The authorities were duly horrified, but I had secured my foothold and was determined not to let it go. I plunged in cheerfully, determined to learn from my mistakes, and I made plenty. At the end of a year's efforts I discovered myself with a few lengths of "OO" gauge track over which nothing would run without derailing. I had built several wagons which looked rather like matchboxes on wheels, and I had one locomotive which

needed to be prodded firmly with a finger every time one wanted it to start or change direction. In short, I discovered that there was a great deal more to the business of railway modelling than I had imagined. Gone were my dreams of building up a magnificent rail empire within a couple of years, and I began to have an uneasy suspicion that I had gone wrong somewhere.

Clearly it was time for some drastic re-thinking. Obviously complicated track work was not my *métier*. I knew that I was primarily interested in the scenic side of railway modelling, and that I would never be satisfied with a model setting which did not look reasonably realistic. So I had another look at the "Madder Valley", abandoned my ideas of a complicated continuous-run layout, and settled for a model of a branch line terminal and nothing more.

I decided it would have to be in 4 mm scale because that was the smallest scale for which proprietary parts were gradually becoming available, and I wanted to cram as much as I could into my available space. The old, three-rail systems of electrification for model railway layouts were obviously on their way out, so that I had no doubt that my railway would be operated on the two rail system, but I was torn for a long time between the

Side view of "Dunedin" and standard gauge goods wagons. The lorry in the foreground is made up from a war-time Wilson's lorry kit. The miniature figures are "Authenticast" figures from Ireland—really for "HO" gauge, and thus looking a bit small here.

respective merits and demerits of the two gauges available in 4 mm scale, namely "OO", and what later came to be called "EM" gauge. "OO" gauge used equipment built to the scale of 4 mm to the foot but ran it on track with a gauge of 16.5 mm, which was actually correct for 3.5 mm scale. This somewhat curious state of affairs had arisen in Britain before the War, when it was felt that 3.5 mm scale models running on 16.5 mm gauge track (known as "HO") were difficult to model accurately due to the large size of the commercial motors then available, and due to certain inherent difficulties, when modelling British locomotive prototypes, of securing sufficient play for bogie wheels set between cylinders. To obtain the extra room the actual scale was boosted half a millimetre, but to obtain the extra wheel play, the track gauge was left at 16.5 mm. Britain was the only country where this happened. There was little difficulty with motors as far as Continental or American locomotive prototypes were concerned, so elsewhere "HO" remained supreme. In America, those modellers who wanted slightly larger models, and who chose 4 mm scale, ran their trains on a track gauge of 19 mm—which was actually a trifle overscale!

After the War, standard "OO" gauge items were slowly re-introduced by the manufacturers, but some modellers felt that a truer track gauge was now possible, and a track gauge of 18 mm was adopted as standard for the new "EM" gauge. This definitely attracted me, but wheels and track for the new gauge

were very hard to come by, and the modeller who chose to model in "EM" had perforce to do a great deal for himself. It struck me that if one were going to have to make all one's track, and adjust all one's own wheels, it would be almost as easy to model a narrow-gauge as a standard-gauge railway. Indeed, the more I thought about it, the more attracted I became by the idea. Interest in narrow-gauge railways as such was growing, but very little had been done in the modelling field. True, many of the locomotives on John Ahern's "Madder Valley" had been based upon narrow-gauge examples, P. R. Wickham had suggested the idea from time to time, and Sydney M. Moir had had some actual models illustrated in the "Model Railway News." But as far as I knew no one had actually built a complete narrow-gauge layout, in spite of the obvious attractiveness which such a layout might have, and in spite of the obvious advantages of being able to model tight curves and short trains while still remaining true to prototype. Anyway, a few tentative experiments convinced me that there was certainly nothing inherently impossible about the idea. So new plans were drawn up, a new and much more substantial baseboard was erected, and the first tracks made their appearance upon its virgin expanse.

It took about six years for the plans to emerge into concrete reality, but in some ways these were the years during which most fun was had, because, of course, everything was new, everything was a challenge, and I was never quite sure just what was going to happen next. Progress was slow simply because I was never able to devote as much time to my hobby as I should have liked. In the beginning there were school examinations to be passed, then

3

"Douglas" (originally "Dunedin II") hauls a train of vintage C.M.R. stock past a starkly bleak Craig Hill made from dyed medical lint spread over crumpled newspapers. The standard-gauge siding disappearing into the tunnel was for many years the only bit of standard gauge track at Craig and over the years there appeared upon it the most peculiar collection of standard gauge bits and pieces which really had no business at all in Craigshire, but which I was unable to resist acquiring. Practically everything in this photograph is a "first"—my first narrow-gauge locomotive, my first narrow-gauge coach and goods vehicles, my first model building—even my first model tree!

there were years of University studies, and finally a living to be earned. All these things were annoying but unavoidable distractions! I did manage, however, to find time during these years to describe my progress and to develop my modelling ideas in a series of articles which appeared first of all in the "Model Railway News", and then in the "Railway Modeller", which began its life in 1949. These articles also were fun to prepare and it was, I must confess, rather pleasant to discover that other people actually enjoyed reading them. I must also confess that the money which they earned came in very useful during the years of chronic financial shortage, and enabled me to purchase several indispensable items of modelling equipment which I would otherwise hardly have been able to afford!

In later years I was tempted more than once to start afresh and model an actual railway locality—something, for example, like Glenfinnan station and viaduct on the West Highland Railway, or the little terminus of Polton on the one-time Lasswade branch line near Edinburgh. These, I am sure, would make fascinating models, but their scope would naturally be very limited, and in the end I have always returned to the idea of the free-lance layout, even if based upon the practice of some known railway company. In my early modelling days I never really considered any other possibility. The custom of creating an imaginary location for one's model railway layout was well established, and my only concern was what to christen my imaginary narrow-gauge empire. I was tempted to evolve a punning name along the lines of the late John Allen's "Gorre and Daphetid" railroad in America, or John Ahern's "Madder Valley." Or else I could have had a semi-humorous name like R. W. G. Bryant's "Inversnecky and Drambuie" railway. In the end, however, I became deadly dull and serious, and the Craig and Mertonford Light Railway was named simply after two houses which had played an important part in my mother's early life as a children's nurse.

2 An historical digression

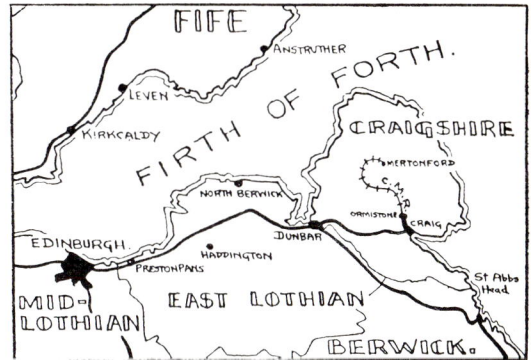

All the best model railways have their history, and the Craig and Mertonford is no exception. The railway is situated almost entirely within the County of Craigshire in south-east Scotland. As the accompanying map shows, Craigshire comprises that part of the Lammermuir Hills lying to the north and east of the main railway line between Dunbar and Berwick-upon-Tweed. (If the reader is unable to find it on any other map that is no concern of mine.) The Craig and Mertonford Light Railway is the only railway serving the remote townships in the Craigshire Hills, but the county town of Craig itself is, of course, on the "Craigshire Deviation" of the main East Coast Route. At the turn of the century both the North British Railway and the North Eastern Railway had running rights over the line, and, quite apart from the through East Coast route express trains there were many local services operated to Edinburgh and the Borders by the N.B.R. and to Berwick and Newcastle by the N.E.R. At one time, moreover, there was a little branch of the Caledonian Railway which managed to infiltrate into the district, but this never developed as the "Caley" hoped it would, and it was quite short-lived. It helped, however, to add to the modelling possibilities of the region!

Lying, as it does, quite far out into the Firth of Forth, Craigshire has had a somewhat less stormy history than the rest of the Lowlands. As already noted, it is a hilly county, and in mediaeval times it was really rather inaccessible. English armies marching north and Scottish armies marching south both tended to ignore it. Battles were fought and lost in the vicinity, but the men of Craigshire tended to hold aloof and to mind their own business. For a long time, indeed, they were more of a liability than an asset to the Scottish kings, and punitive expeditions were periodically sent into Craigshire in an attempt to instil into the residents a sense of what was right and proper. These expeditions never came to very much, since the inhabitants promptly took to the hills and only returned to their villages when the armies had passed by. Nevertheless, several castles were eventually built in various parts of the county,

and in 1316 we find our first reference to the Craigs of Craig when King Robert the Bruce granted the lands of Mertonford to James Craig for somewhat doubtful services rendered on the field of Bannockburn. The charter, for those who are interested, reads as follows, and if anyone cares to hunt for the original in Register House, Edinburgh, he is quite at liberty to do so!

". . . Sciatis nos dedisse concesisse et hac presenti carta nostra confirmasse Jacobo de Craig militi dilecto et fideli nostro totam terram de Mertounforde cum pertinentiis . . . tenendam et habendam eidem Jacobo et heredibus suis de me et heredibus meis in feodo et hereditate bene et in pace livere et quiete et honorifice per servicium dimidii militis . . ."

The "pertinentiis" bestowed in the above charter consisted of the quarries, and, later on, the shale mines, which have always constituted Craigshire's chief source of wealth. These, however, were not worked as extensively as they might have been until the close of the nineteenth century, since they were situated in out-of-the-way places and transport to the coast was always something of a problem.

And so the Craig and Mertonford Light Railway comes into the picture. A railway to connect Mertonford and Craig was proposed as early as 1853, and again in 1876, but nothing came of the idea until Robert, Lord Craig, succeeded to the title in 1894. This particular Lord Craig was quite a go-ahead young man, and in his youth he had paid several visits to North Wales where he had been impressed and delighted by the Festiniog and other narrow-gauge railways of that part of the world. It was, therefore, a foregone conclusion that any railway between Craig and Mertonford would be a narrow gauge affair. Besides, Lord Craig was a true Scot, and everything led him to believe that it would be much cheaper to construct a narrow gauge rather than a standard gauge railway.

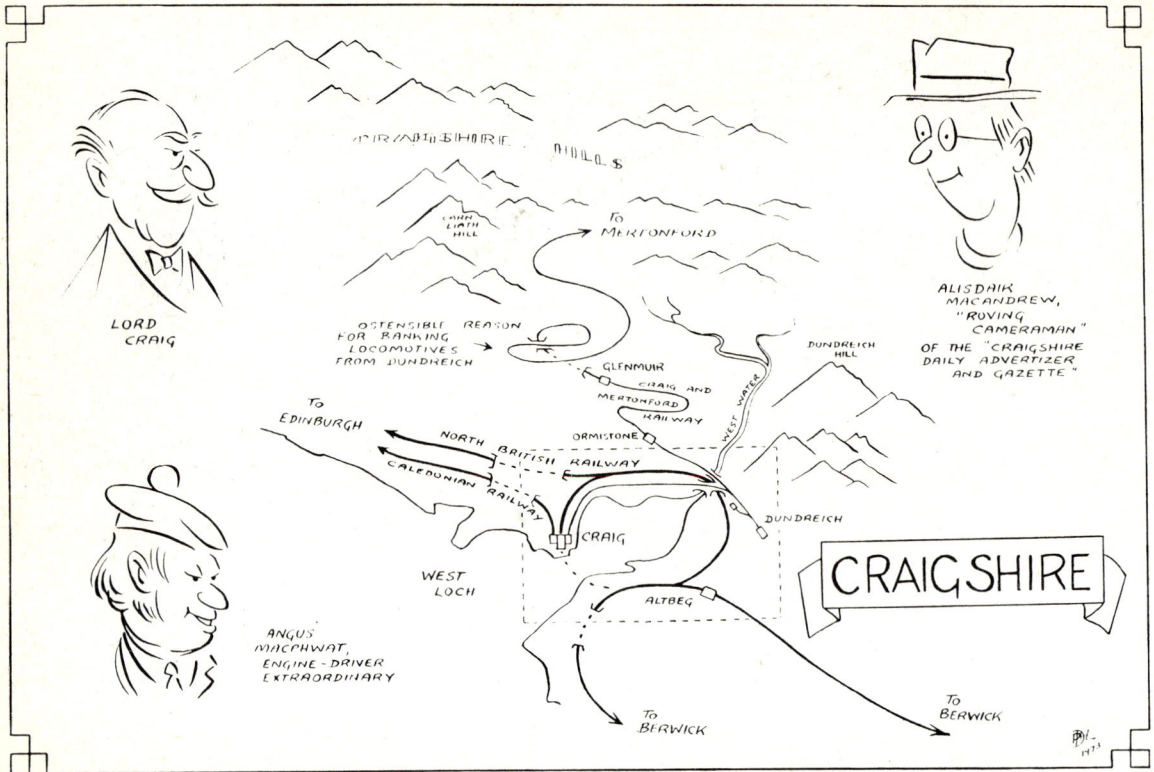

Just exactly how Craigshire fits together may be a bit confusing to some readers—especially if they have read the slightly conflicting accounts which have appeared from time to time in the pages of the "Railway Modeller". I have, therefore—and after much effort—managed to concoct this "official" plan which shows just how the various standard gauge lines link up with the C.M.R. at Craig.

So work on a 2 ft 3 in gauge line was begun in the summer of 1896. A little contractor's engine was bought from Andrew Barclay & Co. Ltd., and the narrow gauge rails began to creep inland towards Mertonford. The whole enterprise turned out to be considerably more expensive than Lord Craig had anticipated, and the following year work was abandoned with the line only half way to nowhere. However, in 1899 Lord Craig had an unexpected windfall as the result of a little flutter on the Stock Exchange, and the end of the year saw the railway finally reach Mertonford. It was a great occasion. Flags and bunting festooned the mine buildings, Lady Craig assisted in the ceremony of driving home the gold spike, and the present Lord Craig, then six years old, was permitted to ride on the footplate of the first official passenger train to arrive from Craig.

It was an auspicious beginning, and for some years the little line prospered. It reached the peak of its prosperity just before the 1914–18 War, and then the decline set in. It was the usual narrow-gauge story. The demand for stone from the quarries dwindled and the shale seams began to peter out. Moreover, the Craigshire roads had been improved and some of them even tarmacadamed. The S.M.T. bus company began to run regular services to Mertonford. It looked like the beginning of the end, but the C.M.R. managed to stagger on somehow until the outbreak of the Second World War. During the war an occasional train brought down stone from the quarries at Mertonford, but, generally speaking, the line was abandoned, and it would probably have closed altogether after the War had it not been for Lord Craig's determined efforts to popularize Craigshire as a tourist resort. You know the sort of thing: "Craigshire—Highland grandeur in the heart of the Borders—explore the beautiful Craigshire Hills by the picturesque narrow-gauge railway—the holiday in Craigshire you'll never forget! etc., etc."

The fact that the C.M.R. remained unnationalized was a great help in this campaign. Probably, as

seemed to be the case with the Tal y Llyn, the authorities had simply forgotten that it had ever existed. Anyway, the brochures which Lord Craig had printed and distributed to the travel agencies all helped to bring visitors to the region, and the visitors travelled on the railway, and things gradually began to pick up. In 1954 a chronicler was found to record developments on the line in a magazine called the "Railway Modeller," which had a considerable sale amongst the ever-growing fraternity of railway enthusiasts. Soon Lord Craig—and even local worthies such as engine-driver Angus McPhwat and Alisdair MacAndrew, the "roving cameraman"— found themselves well-known figures far beyond the confines of their native Craigshire. What really turned the tide was the reopening in 1958 of the shale mines at Dundreich. This assured a commercial as well as a tourist-based future for the railway, and at the time of writing the line remains in a more prosperous condition than it has done for several decades. "We are confident," said Lord Craig at last year's shareholder's annual meeting, "that our little railway will continue to thrive and prosper, and I am happy to inform you that malicious rumours to the effect that we are thinking of purchasing a diesel locomotive are quite without foundation. We tried that some years ago, and we know what happened then, don't we?* (Cheers and laughter!) Whatever British Railways choose to give us to get to Edinburgh—and I don't see why it can't be a three-car instead of merely a twin-car D.M.U.—you may be sure that as long as I remain Chairman of the Craig & Mertonford Light Railway the echo of the steam engine's exhaust will be heard in our Craigshire hills." (Thunderous applause!)

* See: The tale of a diesel; a story with a moral. The "Railway Modeller." October 1955, pp. 226–227.

3 The early years

The room in which all this materialized is 12 ft by 10 ft (3.5 m by 3 m), and, as already mentioned, it has to serve me as a bedroom as well as a model railway room. This, I suppose, has certain advantages as well as disadvantages, although it is sometimes hard to appreciate them. It means, for example, that things have to be kept a good deal cleaner and tidier than would be necessary in a room devoted entirely to the railway. All tools and modelling equipment have to be put properly away at the end of each evening's activities if only because the main work-bench is a large drawing-board on top of the bed! The narrower sections of the railway are carried very conveniently and tidily on top of sectional bookcases, and part of the front of the main base-board is decently draped by slide-along curtains. Small parts are contained in an office-type nest of drawers which stand by one side of my bed, and tools are in a wooden cabinet by the window. Things do pile up and get untidy from time to time, and then hints and warnings from the household authorities force a proper tidying-up and spring-cleaning session upon me. The layout has already had to be dismantled once in order to allow the room to be redecorated, and the same traumatic experience lies ahead of it in the near future. Indeed, one of the reasons for writing this book now is that phase two of the layout's history is now drawing to an end, and this seems a suitable occasion to think things over before embarking upon phase three.

The greatest disadvantage of having the layout in a bedroom is that of bedroom dust and fluff, which physically impedes the running of trains within a remarkably short time unless attended to. Some things can be dusted with the aid of a small brush, but the only way really to clean the layout and get rid of the dust is to use the various attachments that go along with a vacuum cleaner. That thing which is used for poking down the sides of chairs is the most invaluable attachment of the lot. It can be run along between

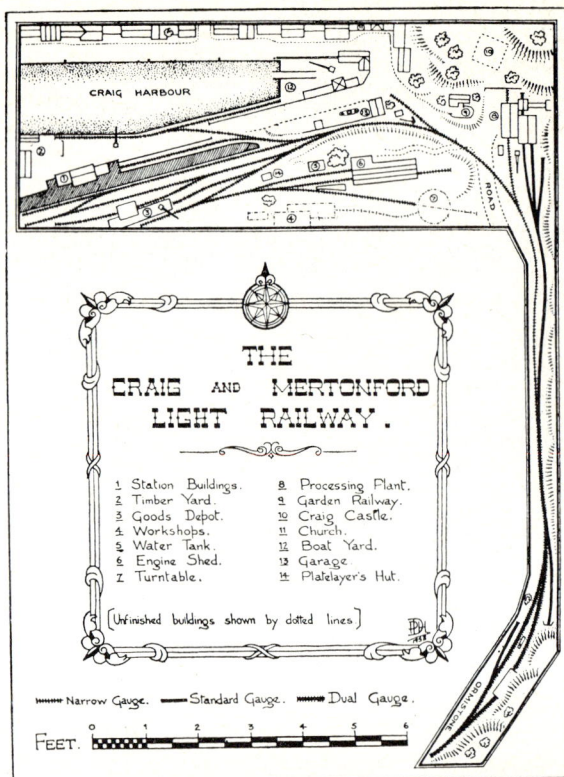

THE CRAIG AND MERTONFORD LIGHT RAILWAY.

1 Station Buildings.
2 Timber Yard.
3 Goods Depot.
4 Workshops.
5 Water Tank.
6 Engine Shed.
7 Turntable.
8 Processing Plant.
9 Garden Railway.
10 Craig Castle.
11 Church.
12 Boat Yard.
13 Garage.
14 Platelayer's Hut.

[Unfinished buildings shown by dotted lines]

Narrow Gauge. — Standard Gauge. Dual Gauge.

FEET. 0 1 2 3 4 5 6

A quiet corner of the original layout. The Cotswold-style house has come to rest beneath the slopes of Craig Hill, Craig parish church has made its first appearance, and the monumental rubbish dump behind the locomotive shed has begun to form at the bottom left of the picture.

Craig had really begun to take shape by the time this photograph was taken. True, there is no station building as yet, but at least a complete Harbour Street has grown at the back of the layout, even if some of the buildings do not look too happy next to each other. There is no Craig Castle, but the boat-building yard has made its appearance, and close examination reveals that "Alistair" and "Ian" have now been joined by "Duncan" and "Angus". Alas, however —the remains of "Douglas" languish behind the locomotive shed.

In the bay platform there is an American-style coach with a raised guard's cupola. It is strange that this coach should appear in so few photographs, since it gave yoeman service in the early days before passing out of my hands into those of Mr. Maurice Broom, upon one of whose layouts it may actually still be running.

The Brigantine "Condor" has some of her sails set in this picture, but somebody or other pointed out to me that this was rather inappropriate for a ship at rest in harbour, so they were later furled and have remained so ever since. The little cabin cruiser on the slipway at the far side of the harbour is a model of the cutter which plays such a prominent part in Arthur Ransome's children's book, "We Didn't Mean to go to Sea".

the rails and poked into odd corners where nothing else will go. A really thorough vacuuming session can take a whole evening, but when it is over it is worth it to see the colour that has reappeared in the Craigshire hills and the gleam that has come back to the tops of the rails.

The basic shape and idea of the layout has remained pretty constant over the years. The first plan published in the "Railway Modeller" for April 1954 shows the town of Craig with harbour, main street, castle, boatyard, processing plant and spacious narrow-gauge station. For many years it was a pretty uncluttered layout, which is not surprising since everything was in the process of being built up. Large areas were covered with medical-lint "grass-land", Craig Hill was covered only by a few sparse trees, and a bare minimum of buildings dotted the landscape. The result was not at all unattractive. Indeed, I feel that some of the photographs taken during those days convey the narrow-gauge "atmosphere" somewhat better than those taken in later years when Craig had become more developed. In the first years, mind you, there only *was* the narrow-gauge railway to contend with, and the only standard-gauge was a short length of line added more to point the contrast than anything else. In other words, the difficulties of trying to blend a proper standard-gauge line plus a tramway into the scene had simply not yet arisen.

The standard-gauge line was treated very cavalierly, being nothing more than a length of dual-gauge track which ran from Craig Processing Plant (Peter Allan's) to Ormistone along a narrow shelf running along one length of the room, above the head of the bed, and ending up above the fireplace mantlepiece. Ormistone was a most undistinguished hamlet in the Craigshire Hills with no houses in sight and nothing at all obvious to justify the dual-gauge run-round which existed there. Just before the run-round a short spur ran into a tunnel which ostensibly led to Dunbar but in reality terminated in a 3 ft long siding concealed in the hills.

The idea was that the standard-gauge goods train would be concealed here. During a lull in the more important narrow-gauge operations it would draw out on the main line and back into the Ormistone run-round. The loco would uncouple, run round its train, detach the end wagons and brake van and propel them into a short siding to be "unloaded." The loco would then push the rest of the train along the main line to the processing plant and wait there while its trucks were loaded up and while a little more narrow-gauge activity took place. Eventually the standard-gauge train would awake to life again, rumble back to Ormistone, collect the wagons it had left there, and vanish once more into the tunnel ready for the whole cycle to be repeated. There was nothing very much in this operation, but it did give

*Craig Hill as it was just before the standard-gauge develop-
ments began to intrude upon the scene. In some ways
this was a more satisfying picture from the scenic point of
view than I managed to achieve for many a long year
afterwards. It has a certain uncluttered spaciousness which
was bound to disappear when I tried to fit more into the
layout. In this picture, Craig Hill is still just on the edge
of the town and retains a distinct rural flavour. However,
as we progress through this book we will see it becoming
more and more submerged under the encroaching town and*

*railway developments—not, I trust, losing its character
altogether.*

*Here "Alistair" pulls the early morning Goods past
Peter Allan's processing plant, and blocks the road for
Sandy MacTavish in his milk trap. There is a good broad,
unfenced field in the immediate foreground—a grand place
for children to play (there are a couple with their father,
down there on the left), or for farmer Andrews to leave a
couple of tethered ponies to graze. It also seems to be a
good place for the C.M.R. to dump its unwanted rubbish.*

the excuse to play about with odd bits and pieces of
standard-gauge equipment, and the sequence of
operations was quite pleasant to watch.

Nevertheless, there was something not quite
"right" about the appearance of the track layout at
Ormistone and several other arrangements were tried
out over the years. The one that lasted longest saw
the disappearance of both the run-round and the
concealed siding. It was assumed that a tunnel at the
Processing Plant end of the line was the one now
leading to Dunbar, and all that remained at Ormistone
were a couple of short sidings, one for standard-gauge
and the other for narrow-gauge vehicles. Room was
also found for a small standard-gauge engine depot,
but there was still very little real interest in the
standard-gauge as such. Indeed most of the locomotives which did operate on the standard-gauge

were actually American types, such as a Mantua
"Booster" 0-6-0 (much the same as no. 72 on the
present Keighley and Worth Railway), a Varney
"Casey Jones" 4-6-0, and a Rivarossi 0-6-0. This was
part of a fascination for the Transatlantic scene which
might have had far-reaching consequences upon the
subsequent development of Craigshire had it not
been supplanted in a year or two by a growing interest
in the British pre-Grouping railways. It is true that
the American locomotives did bear British Railways
or L.N.E.R. insignia, but this fooled nobody, and
there was a very real danger for a time that Craig
might have become Craigsville and the whole locale
might have been moved a few thousand miles west-
wards into Colorado or somewhere! A slight easing
of the danger came when it was decided to create the
Craigshire "Northern Light Railways" in order to

Two views of Peter Allan's Processing Plant in its original form. Peter Allan's is the focal point of the Craigshire shale mining industry. It is to here that the C.M.R. brings the shale from the mines in the Craigshire hills, and it is from here that crude, partly refined shale oil and other products are shipped overseas or else transported by the standard-gauge railway to the final refining plants at Winchburgh or Pumpherston in West Lothian.

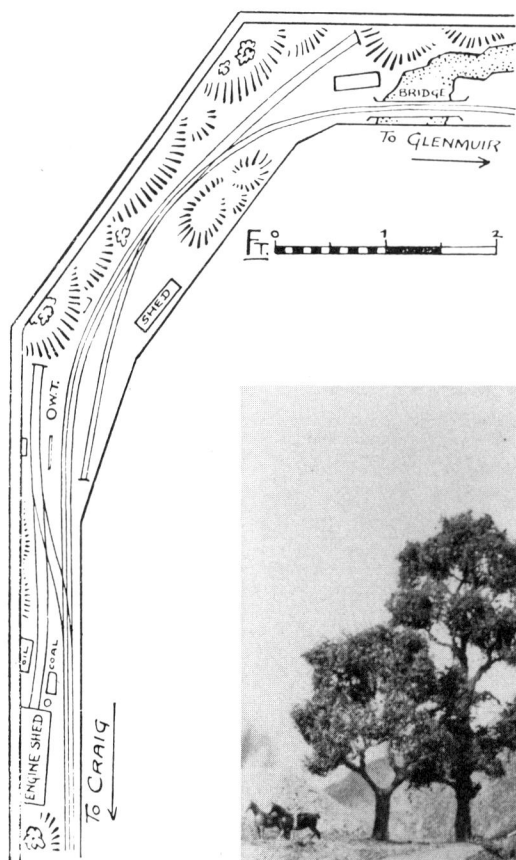

account just a little bit more plausibly for this odd collection of standard-gauge locomotives.

Meanwhile the narrow-gauge C.M.R. had been forging ahead by leaps and bounds. It too was strongly affected by the Transatlantic influence, but when it at last succeeded in circling the room it did so via

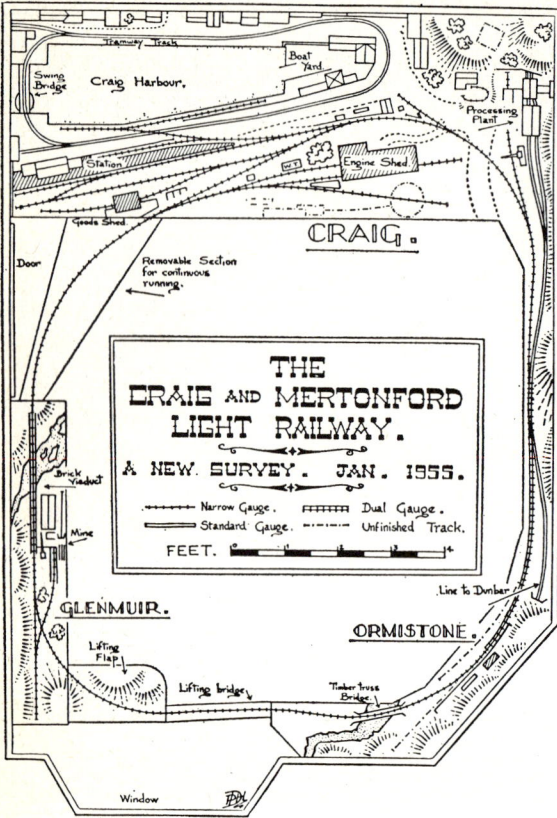

THE
CRAIG AND MERTONFORD
LIGHT RAILWAY.

A NEW SURVEY. JAN. 1955.

Narrow Gauge.   Dual Gauge.
Standard Gauge.   Unfinished Track.

FEET.

Glenmuir—another of the soberly Scottish hamlets in the Craigshire Hills. Glenmuir was supposed to be the location for one of the shale mines which supplied the C.M.R. with one of its reasons for existence. It was really the excuse for a bit of scenic modelling involving a viaduct, a waterfall, a turbulent river and a flight of plastic wood swans. It was also the new terminus of the C.M.R., although the line was supposed, of course, to carry on for many more miles through the hills towards a mythical and never-to-be-materialized Mertonford. However, Glenmuir was now so close in physical reality to Craig that it was impossible to resist the temptation to build a removable "lift-in" section to carry the line past the bedroom door and thus provide the possibility of a continuous run for those occasions when the management got a fit of devilry and felt that it wanted the C.M.R. locomotives really to show their paces for a bit.

The extension of the line from Ormistone necessitated the construction of a new section about three feet long sitting on top of a bookcase and carrying the rails as far as the room window. A lifting bridge attached to the end of the section met up with a hinged flap attached to the Glenmuir section and thus got over the window difficulty. Glenmuir itself

Two views of Ormistone under construction. Although it was once the end of the line, there was never anything very much at Ormistone beyond a run-round or a couple of sidings. It was, however, the place which afforded most opportunity for experimenting with dual-gauge trackwork—track, that is, which could be used by both standard and narrow-gauge stock. Such a track could be achieved either by laying the two rails for the narrow-gauge within those for the standard-gauge—giving a four rail track—or else by utilizing one outer rail for both narrow and standard-gauges and simply laying a third rail. This latter was the easier and more economic method to adopt, although it did not look so good, since people could mistake the inner third rail for an

electric centre rail and ask, "What, still using the three-rail system of current collection?" However, the fact that pointwork was so much easier with the three rail method invariably tipped the balance. Indeed, in one direction it was possible to lead a narrow-gauge track off the dual-gauge track by means of a perfectly ordinary turnout, and it was only where both narrow gauge rails had to cross completely over one of the standard gauge rails that complications arose—as witness the pointwork in the left-hand photograph. The standard gauge locomotive in the second photograph is an American Mantua "Booster"—an illustration of the very real threat there was at one time that Craigshire might have ended up in the Wild West instead of remaining in Scotland.

The bare, bleak hills at Ormistone. In the beginning there really was nothing at all at Ormistone except a single little shed. . . .

Later on, a platform and small station building were added, together with a crane for dealing with freight traffic.

sat on top of two more bookcases on the far side of the room. I flattered myself that the whole arrangement blended the railway in remarkably well with the bedroom aspect of the room, but I am not sure if the household authorities agreed with me. There was little doubt, in fact, that what had once been a bedroom with a model railway in it had now become a model railway room which just happened to have a bed in it!

As at Ormistone, the trackwork at Glenmuir was remarkably simple—too simple, maybe, for what was the terminus of a line operated on a point-to-point basis. In a certain sense, however, it was purposely designed in order to make the reversal of a train just about as difficult as possible and thus add to the spice of operation. Sometimes I felt that I had gone too far, because the task of reversing a passenger train of four coaches involved not only the help of two locomotives but also the shuttling to and fro of the coaches for about ten minutes, which was all very fine and enjoyable in its way, but there were times

The first facilities for dealing with locomotives consisted of no more than a small coaling platform (hidden in this photograph by "Agnes") and a water tower. . . .

This simple narrow-gauge turnout from dual-gauge track is in marked contrast to the complex pointwork illustrated in the first photograph of Ormistone. The standard-gauge locomotive is a Rivarossi Italian State Railways 0-6-0 tank. (There really is no excuse for the peculiar things which ran upon Craigshire's standard-gauge tracks in the early days!)

Finally, however Ormistone could boast a locomotive shed, water tower, and many other amenities including electric light as provided by one of those horribly overscale Trix lamp standards.

when I felt I wanted to get things done in a hurry and wished I had installed an orthodox run-round. Plans were actually drawn up for future run-rounds at both Ormistone and Glenmuir, but these never materialized, any more than did a plan for electrifying the narrow-gauge from Craig to Ormistone on a sort of light tramway basis, so that we could have run locomotives similar to those on the Scottish narrow-gauge lines at Kinlochleven or at Winchburgh.

Possibly the main feature of interest in the trackwork at Glenmuir was the diamond crossing where the siding to what was to become the shale mine

Looking down on to the unfinished shale mine workings by Glenmuir Viaduct.

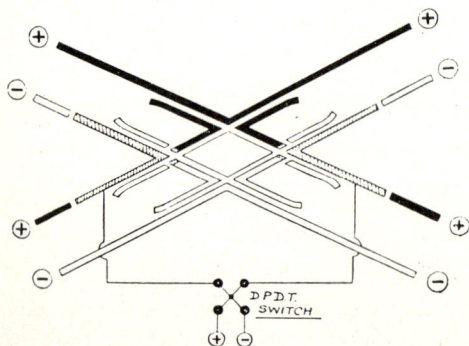

(it never materialized) crossed the main line. Originally the frogs on this crossing consisted of little tufnol blocks, and they were thus completely insulated. This was done in order to simplify construction, but at the slow speeds usual on the C.M.R. locomotives showed a tendency to stall at the crossing so it was rebuilt with live frogs. The only way I was able to make these work was by installing a switch to change the polarity of the frogs as required, but the improvement in running was well worth the labour, and from that time on I decided that all pointwork on the layout would be built with live frogs.

Perhaps it would be as well to mention at this juncture that all trackwork on the original C.M.R. was home-built. In the nineteen-fifties one could not simply go out and purchase a few lengths of Peco narrow-gauge track and half a dozen narrow-gauge points. There was some pioneering work being done at the time in 2 mm scale ("N" gauge, or "OOO" as it was then called) but what was available from H. B. Whall and other suppliers was very basic—one could purchase nickel-silver track "strip" for example—but no ready-made points. There was a difference of opinion, moreover, as to whether 2 mm scale models should run on track of 9 mm or 9.5 mm gauge. I myself had decided on 9 mm gauge for the C.M.R. because some firm, whose name I now forget, had trumpeted itself as "the home of OOO", and had produced a catalogue full of alluring items which promised to be of use to me in my narrow-gauge ventures. Alas—none of these items ever got beyond the planning stage—and when Mr. H. B. Whall began his work, and 2 mm scale items did begin to appear they were all for 9.5 mm gauge, so that I felt that I had chosen wrongly. In the end, of course, commercial "N" gauge equipment appeared using 9 mm gauge track so that my original decision was triumphantly vindicated . . .

My first narrow-gauge track used ordinary "OO" rail spiked directly to the baseboard, with cork ballast packed well up to rail level on the outer sides of the track, and high enough between the rails to cover the pins. This gave the typical half-buried appearance of so many prototypical narrow-gauge tracks, and provided a fairly quick and easy-to-lay method of track construction. The main constructional difficulty was that special slots had to be cut in the baseboard for the point tie rods. It was also a very permanent permanent-way, and alterations

Overall view of Glenmuir viaduct, with unfinished shale mine in the foreground.

were not exactly easy once the track was down. Then PECO small-section conductor rail became available. This was just right for 4 mm scale narrow-gauge and I at once began experiments with it, but came up against the difficulty of wheel flanges hitting against track pins due to the low height of the rail. The eventual method of track construction which was evolved consisted of soldering the rail to pins inserted on the outside of the rail only, but before standardizing on this I became sidetracked by a system whereby the rail was glued by Durofix to specially adapted C.C.W. cork track bases which were then very popular for the construction of super-detailed chaired track. This gave a remarkably realistic track with a certain degree of resiliency which helped to muffle train noises a bit. It was also very much stronger than might have been anticipated, but when things did go wrong it was not always easy to put them right without damaging the cork base. I also evolved a method whereby the polarity of the point frogs was changed by the same switch that operated the point motor—was changed, that is, from the control panel. This did away with any need for switches or special contacts on the point blades and was absolutely foolproof. It may have seemed something like using a sledgehammer to crack a nut, but, really, all that it involved was a little extra wiring, and were I still using point motors on the C.M.R. I think I would be using it now.

At Glenmuir I actually laid the track with ordinary "OO" flat-bottom rail which was spiked to proper wooden sleepers in the best prototypical manner. The rail section was, of course, far too large for any self-respecting narrow-gauge railway, but this was really surprisingly unnoticeable, and the final result was a very pleasing length of track laid on rotting, uneven sleepers, with spikes on every sleeper and Welsh moss and sea-fern "grass" growing up between the rails. It was not such a quiet track as the cork-based track at Craig, but then just how noisy a model railway should be when it is operating is a matter of opinion. Sometimes I even felt that the running at Craig was a little bit too quiet, and at Glenmuir things sounded more or less right so long as speeds were kept at their usual scale 15 to 20 mph—quite fast enough for a supposed 2 ft 3 in gauge line.

I must confess that I have always had a kind of phobia about slow-running on model railways. The slower the better as far as I am concerned! I used to get a great deal of quiet satisfaction watching—and hearing—a train of wagons and small hoppers jolting up the line from Ormistone to Glenmuir. Well, perhaps "jolting" is not quite the right word—my trackwork was not as bad as all that! But at least the wagons clattered and swayed as they passed over the points, the wheels squealed protestingly as the train heeled into the tight curve, and the locomotive began to pant as it tackled the gradient accidentally built into the bridge joining the Ormistone section to Glenmuir. Began to pant, did I say? Yes, that is quite correct. Nearly all the C.M.R. locomotives have some peculiar mechanical deficiency—perhaps the worm wheels are not concentric or something—which gives them quite a pronounced "chuff" when they are running slowly. This, allied to the "clanking"—faint but audible—of the valve gear and connecting rods, gives a rather realistic effect. The valve gear clanks, by the way, and the wagon wheels

Above: A general view of the station approaches in the days when there was nothing else except the narrow-gauge C.M.R. at Craig. Among the street vehicles can be seen a couple of ancient Dinky Toy double-deck buses and a slightly over-scale army searchlight lorry—items which, I believe, have now acquired a certain scarcity value in the eyes of collectors of early die-cast toy motor vehicles. But it's no use anyone writing to ask if they are available for sale, since they have long since departed from the Craigshire scene and passed out of my hands.

Facing page, top: "Alistair" creeps gingerly on to the loading trestle at the side of Glenmuir viaduct. The warning lamp at the end of the trestle signified simply, "no further!" At the foot of the trestle was a small stub of narrow gauge track coming out of a tunnel in the hillside and running a little way along the side of the river. It was intended to develop this as a small shale mine, but the idea never got much further than a good intention.

squeak because they are unoiled. In my very early railway modelling days I used to oil both motion and wheels, but I soon got completely fed up with the task of unwinding oiled-up hairs and fluff from axles and pivot pins, and for many years now the only parts of the C.M.R. stock which have received any oil are the locomotive worms and worm wheels. This has reduced wagon maintenance to the periodic cleaning of wheels and an occasional blowing away of dust, while the locomotives sound (with a bit of imagination) just like the real thing. Admittedly there is a bit more friction to be overcome in getting a train away than there would be if the wheels were all freshly oiled, but then this friction remains constant,

Right: Glenmuir itself—little more than a spot in the wilderness where trains occasionally deign to halt. There are a couple of trees, the shale mine siding, a water standpipe, and really very little else. However, the sun is shining and everything is looking at its best in this photograph as "Alistair" prepares to get the train under way again after a request stop. The driver is just climbing back into his cab after having helped Davie Gilmore to alight. That's Davie there, hobbling away from the leading coach. He's Glenmuir's oldest inhabitant—ninety-three if he's a day—and he's a direct crib of John Allen's "rheumaticky old man", made in the same way from wax brushed on to a wire frame. The "smoke" being blasted out of "Alistair's" chimney would have looked a bit more realistic had I moved the top of the cotton-wool plume around a bit more during the photographic time-exposure.

16

Above and facing page: Early views of Craig locomotive shed, with the whole of the line's motive power on view. "Alistair", "Angus" and "Ian" stand on the service tracks, while "Duncan" potters around with a few wagons. In the engine shed siding an American caboose waits to be attached to a train. This vehicle is used by the C.M.R. as an ordinary brake van, and is one of a number of American-style vehicles which Lord Craig acquired cheaply from a bankrupt Amusement Park firm which had been trying to create an exciting "Wild West" atmosphere for its patrons.

whereas the running of oiled stock in my "bedroom conditions" tended to deteriorate day after day until it became well nigh hopeless and I just had to get down to it and have a spell of axle cleaning. No doubt the friction caused by unoiled bearings could be harmful if the stock were to be run for hour after hour—but then it never is on the C.M.R.—and I shall always know to stop as soon as I see smoke and sparks rising from the wheels of a train!

There has never, by the way, been anything at all fancy about the electric wiring of the layout. Current from the house mains is fed to the layout via a Shenphone rectifier which reduces it to the standard 12 volts. After that, I feed the electricity in at one rail, it passes through the appropriate parts of the electric motor in a model locomotive, moves it along, and comes back out of the other rail! It is all most mysterious. I do not understand how it works but am content that it does. I have one basic rule for wiring, which is that the current must always be fed in at the toe end of a point and never allowed to reach it via the frog. Sidings are no trouble, but as soon as the track leading from one point meets that coming from another point gaps must be installed in the rails. Provided I am ultra cautious about this, and don't attempt anything fancy like "common-return" wiring, everything usually works out all right in the end, but strange things do happen from time to time. The most memorable occurred during the reconstruction at Ormistone when I somehow or other evolved a track circuit whereby I could have all the controllers off, all the switches off—everything off in fact except the actual mains switch and rectifier—and all I had to do was to place a loco on the track and it would run! I could then throw in as many switches as I liked, and twiddle as many control knobs as I liked, but nothing would stop that loco trundling along. It made a change, mind you, from the more normal state of affairs when I cannot get anything to run at all—but it did make

Close-up of some of the litter and miscellanea around the loco. shed and workshops. There is a cement mixer and various odd girders stacked against the side of the shed, a wagon-hoist, a turntable, half a dozen wagon and coach bogies and sundry trolleys, wheels, and tools lying around all over the place.

realistic operation rather difficult. I forget exactly how I eventually solved the problem. I think it just sorted itself out as I rebuilt the layout. I know I never succeeded in finding a satisfactory explanation for it. It was probably one of those "short circuits of short circuits" caused by a locomotive on the other side of the room standing on a particular piece of track in

Preparing for the day's work. Another view of "Alistair" and "Angus" taking on coal and water. The ash tree is a rather unusual feature to find in close proximity to a locomotive shed, but it was planted by George IV to commemorate his visit to Scotland, and to Craigshire in particular, in 1822. Lord Craig positively refused to allow it to be cut down when the railway was built, so the tracks were carefully planned to go around it. . . . It certainly helps when your industrial magnate is also a leading Conservationist!

General view of the locomotive shed and Company workshops at their most extensive just before the rebuilding of the layout. Never again would there be so much room available for this feature.

such a way that it completed a circuit via one of the rails upon which it was standing, a crossover just behind it, another locomotive standing in a passing loop ten yards away and a string of wagons with metal couplings which succeeded in bridging a rail gap somewhere. Or something like that!

A later view of the locomotive shed after the coming of the tramway. The C.M.R.'s workshop facilities have expanded enormously, and most of the once vacant ground to the right of the shed has now been taken over by the Company. The children who used to play on the waste ground have thus lost their football pitch, but there is a certain compensation in watching all the railway goings-on, and no one minds if they trespass on railway property. Angus McPhwat keeps an eagle eye on them, and a threat to call the "polis" if they show any signs of misbehaving is quite sufficient to keep them in order. This in itself is a sufficient clue to let us know that the clock has now been turned back to Edwardian times!

4 The year of the trams

The changing face of Craig is shown in this later view of Peter Allan's Processing Plant. The castle has now emerged in its place of honour on top of Craig Hill, and the road past the Plant now crosses the C.M.R. and the new standard-gauge tracks by means of a bridge, instead of by the old unguarded level crossing. What is more, the bridge bears a line of tramway track, revealing how the suburbs of Craig are reaching out into the surrounding countryside. Para-doxically, of course, this scene is still set in the "present day"—as witness the motor bus parked outside Peter Allan's—but plans were already afoot when it was photographed to transport the picture backwards to the Edwardian era.

1956 was the year of the trams. There had been a time in Britain, not so very many years ago, when most towns of any importance at all had their tramway systems. Most of the smaller systems had vanished before the last War but the larger systems survived the war years most successfully, albeit in a somewhat run-down condition. However, the money needed to refurbish and modernize the systems was not forthcoming and there was, anyway, a very strong anti-tramway lobby in the country. Tramways were considered old-fashioned, noisy, and an impediment in the street to the progress of the all-important private motorist. The fact that modern tramway systems were being built on the Continent which were none of these things was conveniently ignored, and the British tramways began to pass rapidly into history. At the start of the nineteen-fifties there were four tramway systems in Scotland—those of Dundee, Aberdeen, Edinburgh and Glasgow. They were abandoned in that order, and by the end of the decade there were none. In 1956 the Edinburgh system had only one more year to run, and so interest in trams was at a sort of fever-pitch amongst those of us interested in such things.

One keen enthusiast was Mr. Nigel Macmillan of Glasgow, who had built a small tramway system as an adjunct to his "O" gauge railway. This intrigued me mightily, and at the next annual meeting Craig Burgh town council voted by seventeen votes to five in favour of scrapping its uneconomical fleet of Dinky Toy buses and investing in a nice old-fashioned tramway.

The result was a single-line tramway track running along Craig harbour front, round the boat-building yard, down past the narrow gauge station, and across the harbour entrance by means of a swing bridge. The system was pretty obviously a traditional oval, but, in an attempt to disguise the fact, a dummy track led off in a "seawards" direction from Harbour Street, and another track branched off to cross the C.M.R. by a road bridge near the Processing Plant. This never got anywhere, but it made a useful siding, and looked very attractive scenically.

Craig Corporation tramcar No. 77, newly built, poses for her photograph. The implication was that there were at least seventy-six other tramcars owned by the Corporation, but, as you can probably guess, No. 77 was the first and only vehicle. Shortly after she was built Craigshire went pre-Grouping, with the result that she was transferred to the Craig and District Electric Traction Co. and renumbered No. 7.

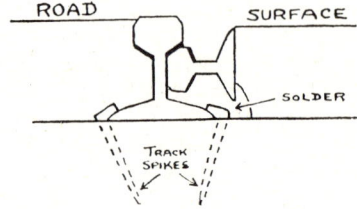

Originally "Craig Corporation Tramways", the system was later rechristened the "Craig and District Electric Traction Co."—a name suggested by David Ronald*, who gave a great deal of active help when it was decided to rebuild the layout to more professional standards in 1957. Harbour Street and the tramway system were then made a self-contained unit, the main part of the system consisting of two parallel tracks running along the harbour front with loops (of ridiculously small radii) at either end. It was really just another continuous-run layout but the effect for most of the way was that of a double line of tramway track with centre poles. There was no attempt to disguise the loop at the Castle end of the system, but at the harbour entrance end the loop was concealed in buildings behind the little tram depot, and it was optimistically hoped that onlookers who saw trams disappearing at one side of the sheds and later reappearing at the other would assume that they were new trams coming from far distant parts of the town!

Two different methods of track construction were used on the layout. The first consisted of "OO"

* Now Major Ronald, Royal Corps of Transport.

flat-bottom rail, with small-section rail laid on its side and soldered into the web of the larger rail, as shown in the illustration above. When the road was built up around the rails this gave a most realistic effect, with the advantage that the road between the running rails was very slightly lower than that outside—thus facilitating track cleaning. The only real disadvantage was that the clearance given for flanges was very "true-scale" indeed, which wouldn't have mattered if David Ronald and I could have relied upon our track being a hundred per cent to gauge—but to expect track to be a hundred per cent to gauge at Craig was perhaps asking too much, so we tried method number two—especially on the curves.

This consisted simply of laying together two lengths of "OO" flat-bottom rail—one rail upright and the other on its side as per the illustration. This method gave a slightly wider flangeway and looked almost as good as the first method, since the somewhat unusual shape obtained at the bottom of the groove turned out to be virtually invisible.

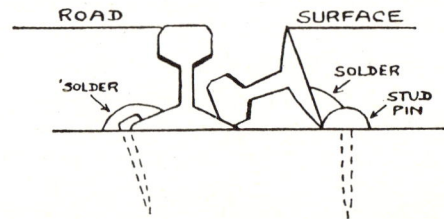

The entire track was inset into the roadway in a most extravagant and laborious way—more by accident than design. After pondering the pros and

Where tramway met narrow-gauge. An impressive view of the trackwork at the approaches to Craig Station, with a good view of the engine-shed puddle.

Do you remember the sound of tramcars in our streets? It is a sound which can still be heard in Blackpool, of course— and in Glasgow the sound of a passing "blue train" can sometimes awaken nostalgic memories—but for most of us the sound is one that can be heard only on gramophone records or on visits to the Continent. Even model tramcars do not always sound like the real thing. Fortunately, however, No. 77 had a Romford motor with just the right degree of whine to impersonate a typical Edinburgh tramcar with a motor long overdue for replacement. Here No. 77

cons of cardboard inlays, plaster of Paris and other odd media, we tried the experiment of insetting a small section of the track with plastic wood, and, while the stuff was still gooey, embossing granite setts upon the surface with the aid of a screwdriver. The result looked beautiful, and in a rash moment we decided to inset the whole track by this method. We calculated that it would not take more than three tins of plastic wood and ought not to take so very long. Come to think of it, I don't suppose it really did take such an inordinate length of time, but by the time we had finished spreading plastic wood between the rails, and had embossed the 10,999th granite sett—well, it *felt* like years! Mind you, the finished track did look rather nice. It is still there, permanently —very permanently—inset into the roadway, and any future track alterations will need to be conducted with the aid of a 4 mm scale pneumatic drill.

There are only four points on the system, and these are "sprung" in proper tramway fashion so as to offer pre-selected routes to tramcars coming in opposite directions. The main point leading into the depot has only one moving point blade. A light spring normally keeps this pressed against the stock rail as shown below, and tramcars coming from A to B2 thus automatically take the curved line, while tramcars coming along the straight line from B1 to A simply push open the point blade as they pass.

The other points have no moving blades at all. The flangeways where the point blades would normally be were filled up with plastic wood, and when this had hardened they were opened up again with the aid

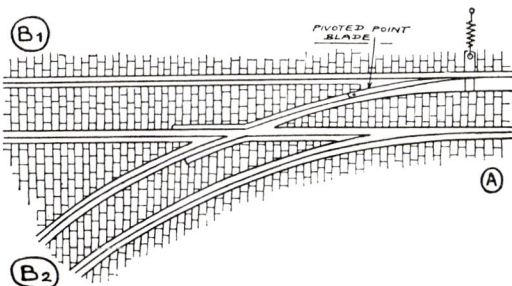

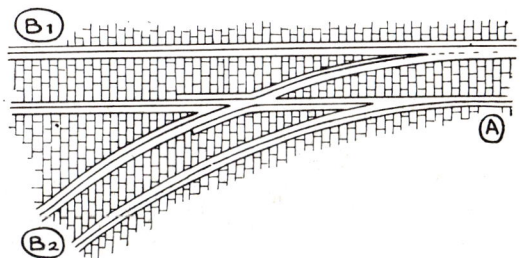

The original tramway circuit went right round the harbour. Here No. 77 trundles along Craig waterfront. . ..

. . . past Craig Church and round by the boatbuilding yard. . . .

. . . and eventually back over the harbour entrance bridge.

of a fine file—but only so far! The "preferred" route from A to B (that is the route which the trams were normally to take) was opened out to its full depth, but the other route was opened out only partially. Thus where the normal route was to be from A via the curved track, then the curved flange-

way was opened out fully and the other, being higher, automatically forced the wheels of a vehicle into the curve. Tramcars coming from B1 to A just bumped over the raised flangeway. This may sound a bit alarming, but it was found that only a very small difference in depth between the two flangeways was needed, and the bumping of trams over the raised flangeway is hardly noticeable when one is watching operations. Anyway, a little jolting and swaying all helps to create the proper well-remembered tramway atmosphere!

The first C. & D.E.T. Co. tramcar was a free-lance affair originally numbered 77, and later reduced in the ranks to no. 7. This was simply a home-built tram body mounted on top of an adapted Romford motor bogie, which was fitted with 9.5 mm diameter "TT" gauge wheels and suitably doctored sideframes. It might have been possible to solder the various tramcar bits and pieces on top of the original side frames after they had been filed flat, but I was afraid of melting them, so they were drilled and tapped in a number of places for 10 and 12 B.A. screws and the new fittings were soldered to these. The tram body itself was built up out of sheet brass and Mr. H. B. Whall's "OOO" gauge rail strip. Curved staircases of the traditional sort were rather funked, and straight stairs fitted instead. For an experimental vehicle no. 7 was satisfactory enough and she is still in service, although looking a bit tatty now beside the later vehicles, nos. 2 and 3.

No. 2 is the pride of the fleet, and she took quite a time to build. She is a typical open-top car of late Victorian or early Edwardian vintage with lots of nice fiddly detail on the top deck—a little bit more uncomfortable for the citizens of Craig, perhaps, than a modern totally enclosed car, but you can't have everything. Lord Craig likes it, and that's what counts at the Company board meetings!

The truck frames of no. 2 are Peckham-type lost-wax brass castings as retailed by Mr. Meadowcroft of Colne, Lancashire, and the motor (which forms an integral part of the underframe) is a home-built affair utilizing the armature and magnet from an old Zenith motor bogie. Originally only one axle was driven directly by worm and worm-wheel by the motor, and a flywheel was fitted on the other end of the armature shaft. The axles were connected by an elastic band running over pulleys. This was an experiment necessitated partly by the fact that only one

C. & D. E. T. Co. tramcars No. 2 and No. 3 passing each other in Harbour Street. I'm afraid we can't explain away the anachronism in this photograph—at least, I'm pretty sure they never built cars in 1912 like that one standing outside Martin's Stores.

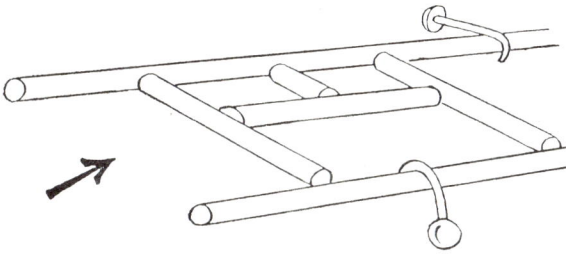

set of the original Zenith worm and worm-wheels was available—the other having already been used in one of the C.M.R.'s more peculiar locomotives, "Duncan". However, it was not a particularly successful experiment, and in due course "Duncan" was rather ruthlessly dismembered largely so that the worm and worm-wheel could be extracted and donated to tramcar no. 2.

The window frames for no. 2 were actually soldered up from individual pieces of brass wire. The two main lengths of wire were held flat upon a plain block of wood with the aid of bent pins as shown in the illustration, and the other pieces were held in position with the aid of tweezers while the soldering iron

C. & D. E. T. Co. tramcar No. 2 was a much better vehicle in every way than No. 77—from the point of view of modelling craftsmanship that is. The passengers who had to sit on the top deck might have thought a little bit differently when it was raining. On the other hand, they would enjoy the sunshine and fresh air on a good day. The poster for Payne's Poppets might be thought to be an anachronistic advertisement for a certain type of confectionery, but it is just conceivable that it might be advertising a rather daring revue showing at the Craig Alhambra theatre.

was brought into play. This left little fillets of solder at each joint, and when the whole assembly was filed flat these became quite respectable rounded corners. The prospect of filing everything flat was a little alarming, but in the event the job proved quite straight-forward and nothing broke apart. The secret turned out to be to file at an angle to all the joints—that is in the direction indicated by the arrow in the illustration.

I am proud to say that I did attempt proper curved staircases for no. 2. They may not bear very close inspection, but they are not exactly impossible, and

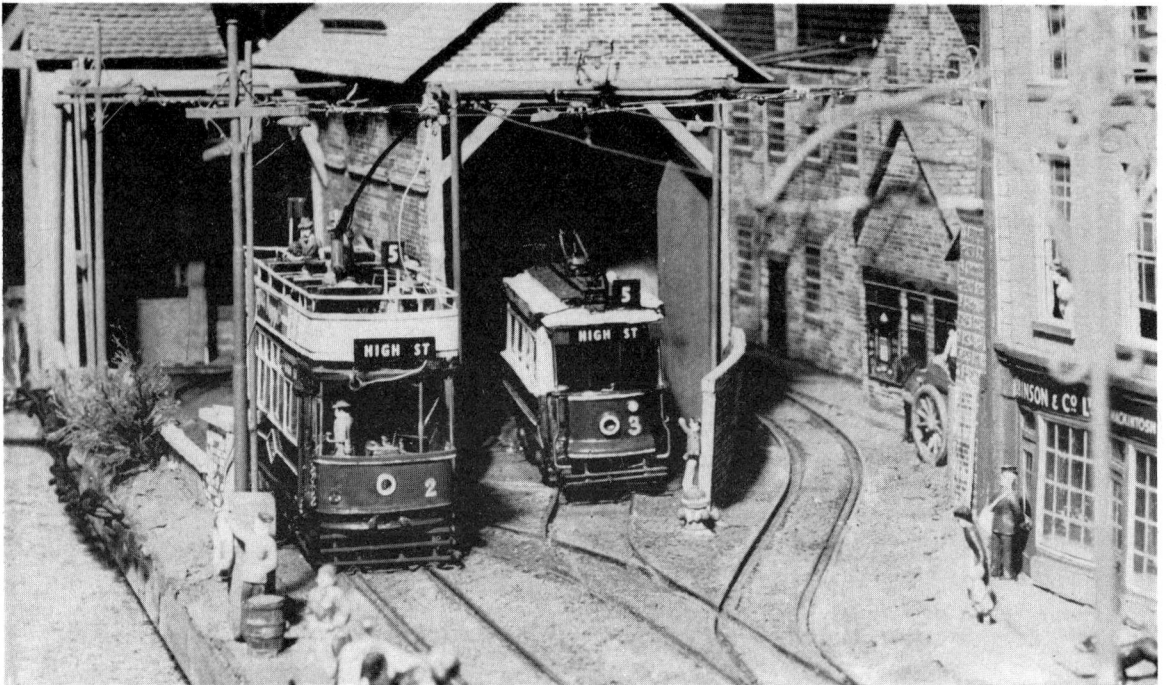

The tram depot. The sharpness of the curves is worthy of note—trams can get round square corners. .

they are the best I was able to achieve after about half a dozen attempts. The method of construction—even now that they are made—still remains something of a mystery to me. It has something to do with twisting the inner side of the stairway into a figure eight, curving the outside one equidistantly around it, and soldering in little triangular steps. The reader can try it for himself if he wants to go quietly crazy!

The seats on the top deck were child's play in comparison. They were formed out of little bits of brass wire bent to shape with the aid of small pliers, and with slats, cut from thin veneer wood, glued in position to form the seats and backs. These are not genuine tip-over seats, but they pass muster at a distance and many of them are half hidden by the passengers (Slater's Huminiatures).

The route numbers and destination boards were cut from magazine advertisements and give a very neat finish. I have been meaning for years to produce a new set of destination boards photographically, and to re-route the trams to Craig Hill and Harbour Street, but meanwhile they are all route no. 5 and all are bound for the High Street.

The tram is painted in the regular C. & D.E.T. Co. livery which is virtually the same as the old pre-war Edinburgh tramcar livery, viz. maroon panels, white window frames and yellow ochre lining on the lower deck, and white side sheets with decorative black lining on the upper deck. The black lining, with its curves and scrolls caused me quite a bit of bother, and I must confess that in the end I cheated. The whole affair was drawn out in Indian ink on a strip of thin white paper which was then glued right round the brass side sheet. After a dozen years in service the white is now more of a cream colour and the maroon paintwork has mellowed considerably, but I think No. 2 is still good for a few more decades before she will need to visit the paint shop again.

Tramcar No. 3 was a purchase from Mr. P. J. Walker of Birmingham and was originally an American-type single-decker with sides very similar to those of the San Francisco cable cars. She was anglicized in Craig Works and the opportunity was taken to use up some sample parts from a Ratio tramcar kit. Peckham type sideframes were also fitted to the original truck. Originally she was fitted with a Lindsay L-180 motor. This had a special enclosed gear box which was all very well, but meant that it was well nigh impossible to fit any other than the standard gears, and these drove the car far too

C. & D. E. T. Co. No. 2 passing the tram depot.

rapidly for a self-respecting tramcar. A variety of other motors were therefore tried, but none of them were particularly successful and No. 3 obstinately remained one of those models I get from time to time which have nothing obviously wrong with them but which nevertheless persist in "playing up" by running erratically, or derailing, or refusing to start, or otherwise misbehaving. She has now been withdrawn from service and sits in a box along with other discards while the Company ponders what to do with her.

All the tramcars have slightly different trolley heads, in that car No. 7 has a platinum-wire head, car No. 2 a copper head, and car No. 3 a head incorporating a small carbon rubbing block (part, incidentally, of a genuine Edinburgh Corporation tramway trolley head!) Of these three heads the least

efficient is the plain copper one and the most efficient the carbon one. Probably the platinum head would be the best if it were entirely platinum, but, as it is, all that we can afford of this fabulously expensive material is a short length of wire. This, bent as shown, makes contact with the overhead wire at only a few isolated points whereas the carbon block, for example, makes contact over its entire length. Theoretically, therefore, the carbon block head has become our standard type, although, even after all these years, we still haven't got any further in fitting it to the other cars!

The overhead wiring has been carried out using soft copper wire of about 26 swg—the sort of stuff obtainable in most radio shops. This was pre-stretched to try to minimize any tendency to sag, and the insulating enamel on the wire was removed by drawing it several times through folded sandpaper. I experimented with short lengths of phosphor-bronze, nickel silver and other more "springy" wires in the overhead, but none of them seemed to make much difference to the current collection, and were all much more difficult to erect neatly than the soft copper wire.

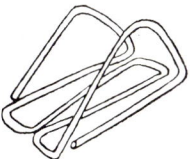

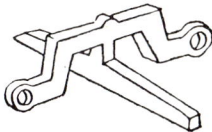

Tramway centre pole in Harbour Street, based upon the type which used to run down the middle of Leith Walk in Edinburgh. The plastic wood "granite sets" have come out quite well in this photograph.

When hanging the overhead wire from the cross spans use was made of a dozen or so little brass hangers which were obtained from the Wagner Car Co. in America. These hangers are actually designed for American gauge "O" ($\frac{1}{4}$ in scale), but they are so small that they look quite at home in 4 mm scale and add a very professional look to the wiring. Other overhead wiring gadgetry has been made from springy copper or bronze wire bent to form pull-offs or other special types of hanger. Where it was necessary to insulate two wires from each other little fibre insulators have been used, each with two holes drilled in them. Overhead frogs are of the simple "pan" type made from sheet brass.

Poles for the overhead wiring are of two types. The centre poles along Harbour Street are based upon those which used to run down the middle of Leith Walk in Edinburgh—lovely examples of "Victoriana" with plenty of nice twiddly bits. These —the twiddly bits—were quite easily formed out of brass wire with the help of a small pair of round-nosed pliers. The only trouble was the time it took to make all the necessary bits and pieces. The different widths on the poles were obtained by wrapping several layers of parcel tape round the main poles at the requisite heights.

The poles at the end of the street, near Craighill, and at the tram depot, are Edinburgh "standard" poles. These poles also carry lights and they were therefore made of fine brass tube so that the necessary wiring could be internal and inconspicuous. One lead was carried up through the pole and the return was via the metal post itself. The bulbs used were an ultra-miniature type as retailed by G. W. Jones Bros and Co. Ltd. of Chiswick, and they were fitted with small reflector shades consisting of 8 B.A. cup washers. All this, incidentally, is in the past tense, because not so long after they were installed I forgot what voltage the bulbs were supposed to operate from and accidentally passed a disastrous 24 volts

Edwardian elegance. Tramcar No. 2 in lonely state at Craighill. The extension of the tramway to Craighill involved the erection of a two arch roadbridge over the C.M.R. and very careful adjustment of the tramway overhead to ensure that the tramcar trolley poles didn't leave the wire as the trams bucked over the bridge. The extension to Craighill was only a couple of yards long, but it added considerably to the interest of operation, and the spectacle of the trams climbing up to the bridge and rattling down the other side was one that never palled.

through the whole system. Not one bulb survived. And since they are all such an integral part of the posts I haven't yet got around to replacing them. The job, in fact, has a pretty low priority amongst all the hundred and one other jobs that are waiting to be done, so the inhabitants of Craig look as though they are going to have to endure their "power cut" for quite a few years to come.

Close up of the overhead wiring showing pan-frog, and some of the Wagner Car Co. brass hangers.

5 The middle years

Parallel with the development of the tramway system at Craig there was a growing interest in the standard-gauge part of the layout. This was due partly to the slow accumulation of bits and pieces of standard-gauge equipment which had nowhere to run, and partly to my own increasing acquaintance with the standard-gauge railways of Scotland and the north of England.

Slowly and insidiously, this interest in the standard-gauge began to demand better representation at Craig. I had no intention of abandoning the narrow-gauge C.M.R., of course, but I did find myself wondering more and more whether something could be done to extend the standard-gauge feeder line and increase the interest of its operation. The most obvious thing to do was to make Craig station into a standard-gauge as well as a narrow-gauge station, but since Craig was already a fully built up area, this meant that something already in existence would have to go, and this would be bound to have repercussions elsewhere. As it turned out, the repercussions proved to be even more far-reaching than I had imagined they might be, and the final result several years later was the complete rebuilding of the layout, and a turning back of the clock to pre-Grouping days.

This period of alteration and adjustment to the original layout lasted well into the early nineteen-sixties, but in spite of the changes Craig remained recognizably the same place. New railway tracks might be laid or old ones lifted, but everything happened around the same harbour, with the same row of buildings in the background, the same boat-building yard at one end of the harbour, the same processing plant busy at one side of it, and the same Craig Castle looming above all. In the end some of these features were to be swept away by the wind of change, but they seemed so permanent for such a long time that no account of Craig during this period would be complete without a closer look at them.

Theoretically the most permanent of them all was Craig Castle. This was one of the features of the layout which had been planned from the very beginning, but it did not really make its appearance until 1957, and its absence until then was always a source of considerable embarrassment, since it was supposed to have been in existence since the Middle Ages!

Looking across to the tram depot on the far side of the harbour. Apart from the "Condor" and a steam tug moored to the far jetty the only other things in the water are the five swans.

Originally the castle was to have been a model of Clackmannan Tower, but in the end the choice fell upon Falside Castle, just outside Edinburgh. This is a somewhat insignificant castle as castles go, but I can see it from my window★, and am rather fond of it. Its only real moment of "glory" occurred in 1547

★ Not quite so well now as in 1957, since the view is now partly obscured by a couple of blocks of "high-rise" flats.

when the battle of Pinkie was fought around its walls. However, from the modelling point of view, it possesses the positive virtues of being reasonably picturesque, typically Scottish, and small enough to fit into the vacant space on top of Craighill.

When I did finally get down to building it the model went together surprisingly quickly. The walls are of thick card—old photographic mounting boards, in fact—and these are braced internally with a selection of ruined walls, staircases and floor beams. No

First attempts at amalgamating narrow and standard gauge at Craig were not altogether successful. This photograph probably illustrates Craig at its most cluttered and unconvincing.

available stone paper seemed to be quite right for the walls, so the stonework was drawn in and painted by hand. The model is of the castle as it was in 1957, and it has actually worn better than the original, which has now lost a good deal more of its rather fine gable end, and has only narrowly escaped being demolished altogether by the Philistines!

The grounds around the castle have always been considered to be part of the municipal park, laid out with pleasant walks and good views of the distant Craigshire Hills. Similarly one of the nearby buildings has always been the town museum where the local citizens and visitors may view many interesting relics of Craigshire's past. Here, a whole room is devoted to the coming of the railway to Craig, and contains photographs of the present Lord Craig's father digging the first sod, presiding at the C.M.R. inauguration ceremony, declaring the Craig and District Electric Traction Co. well and truly open, and performing numerous other similar functions. All these photographs have been generously donated by Lord Craig himself, who also owns the Museum (admission five pence, or one old-fashioned shilling, children half-price, closed on the Sabbath.)

Two views of Craig goods shed, built when the standard gauge reached the town. This shed was quite a pleasant structure, made from North Eastern capped boarding which

was sent to me by a correspondent in the United States, and which gave a most characteristic railway-like appearance to the finished model.

A view of the station approaches taken just before Craigshire went pre-Grouping. In fact, this is just about the closest that Craig ever came to appearing in really modern guise, for the string of hoppers entering the station is now being hauled by "Joan"—the C.M.R.'s one and only venture into the field of diesel traction. The tramway has been banished to the other side of the harbour, and its place is taken by new standard gauge tracks which have even encroached on to space once occupied by the boatyard.

Another establishment which dates from the very early days, and which is actually still with us, is Peter Allan's processing plant. This acquired a certain notoriety over the years simply because it was never revealed precisely what it was that was processed there. All sorts of wild rumours have circulated, of course, and the mystery has now become so long established, and so much part and parcel of Craigshire lore, that it seems a pity to have to break the news that Peter Allan's is probably a shale processing plant. This, at any rate, is the most likely outcome of the acquisition of numerous Eggerbahn hopper wagons and the emergence of a shale mine further along the line. The reader may remember from the historical digression a few chapters ago that shale mining had been envisaged, right from the start, as one of the main reasons for the C.M.R.'s existence. However, for a long time the only hopper vehicles we had were eight or nine rather massive things from Woolworths, and these did not seem sufficient to get the shale mining industry properly under way—even if Peter Allan's processing plant was there all ready and waiting.

The plant buildings were based upon a kit of parts which was advertised in the American "Model Railroader." The original kit consisted of various metal strips and corrugated sheets intended to be soldered together, but my version was concocted from stripwood, Bristol board, and Slater's corrugated card. Over the years it has lost some of its outbuildings and exists at the time of writing in a somewhat curtailed form. However, I do have quite ambitious plans in mind for the Craigshire shale mining industry, and I hope the day is not too far distant when Peter Allan's will be resuscitated in its full glory.

Incidentally, the reason why it is shale mining as opposed to any other sort of industry is simply that in the early nineteen-fifties there was still an extensive shale mining industry in Midlothian, and at Winchburgh there was a fascinating 2 ft 6 in gauge electric railway which I used to enjoy visiting and, occasionally, riding upon! The mines have now closed down, and the little railway has passed away, but I still hanker for something a little more concrete to

33

The boatbuilding yard workshops as they appeared from within the yard. The long box-like object in the foreground is the steam chest for bending planks to shape, and just out of sight under the corrugated iron roofing there is a circular saw contrived out of a watch gear wheel.

The boatbuilding yard crane—just a few strips of balsa wood, some Woolworth's jewellery chain, and a few more small clock gear wheels.

remember it by than mere photographs, and one of these days there is going to be a cable-hauled incline at Peter Allan's, with little hopper wagons rumbling up it, clattering into the plant, and re-appearing minutes later as new trains of empty wagons to be hauled away by "Colin" or "Calum" to Craig harbour, or back to the mines.

Just to the side of Peter Allan's, at the end of the harbour, there used to be quite an extensive boat-building yard, complete with a little fishing boat under construction. The general idea for the yard came from a model on display in the Royal Scottish Museum, Edinburgh, but the Craigshire yard was somewhat modernized, and very much smaller. The workshops were all condensed into the one long building which can be seen in some of the photographic illustrations. It was unfortunate that it was the back of this building which had to face the railway and which was seen by anyone viewing the layout, because it was the *other* side of the building which contained all the detail, including a workshop with circular saw and other tools, a steam chest for bending planks to shape, and assorted piles of timber and other interesting paraphernalia. It seemed a waste of good detail, and I tried various ways of rearranging things so that the building could be on the other side of the yard, but somehow this seemed to spoil the general symmetry of things and I always ended up by putting it back as it had been.

The boat in the stocks started life as a Triang tugboat—and what is more, it used to work. The idea was to present it to a young cousin of mine, and it

RINSELL

was accordingly fitted out with a Rev electrotor,* a couple of pencil-torch batteries, and even a combined rheostat control and reversing lever. The first sea trials (in the placid waters of the nearby bathtub) were satisfactory enough, though it emerged that the rheostat speed control was rather a wasted bit of effort, since the boat had only two speeds—dead slow and stop! However, second trials (in rough water) soon revealed a most sinister defect—the boat was top-heavy! As I stirred the water at the far end of the bath with the loofah, and the first gentle waves slapped against her side, she slowly heeled over and went under with a most delightful plop and a gurgle. This completely ruined the electrotor, and with it my cousin's chances of getting a boat for his birthday. Anyway, I salvaged her, removed her innards, and established her high and dry in the boatbuilding yard.

The yard crane was an old-fashioned derrick made very simply from stripwood, some old watch gears and various lengths of Woolworth jewellery chain which were purchased long before cheap 32-link-per-inch model chain became available. The chain was not painted since this would have tended to clog up the links; instead it was brushed with iodine, which turned it first of all a dull grey, and then, within a few weeks, a nice matt black.

Behind the boatbuilding yard, and a little way up the side of Craighill was the house owned by the manager of Peter Allan's. This was a suburban-type

*An obsolete form of miniature electric motor working on some weird and wonderful principle which was then, and still remains, a complete mystery to me.

Craig boatbuilding yard, photographed presumably from the roof of the narrow-gauge locomotive shed. This is a view of the yard in its earliest and most extensive state, before various railway and tramway developments began squeezing it into an ever shrinking triangle of space. In the very early days the yard was owned by H. Jones & Co. Pty. Ltd., which sounded rather un-Scottish. The trouble was that in those days all my shop and other names came from suitable newspaper, magazine or book jacket cuttings, and at the time the yard was built there was nothing more appropriate available. One would imagine that Scottish newspapers and magazines would be full of suitable Scottish names, but the difficulty is to find them the right size and in white or coloured letters on a black or coloured background. I always intended, of course, to change the name to something more Scottish, but when the yard did change hands the new owner turned out to be a character with the name of "Grinsell"! Honestly—I really couldn't have been trying very hard. . . .

The fishing boat shored up and under construction in the yard is of the type commonly seen around the Craigshire coast, with the deck house a little bit further forward than is usual on Scottish fishing boats. The hull is that of a Tri-ang model tugboat, and the deck house is built up from C.C.W. wooden coach construction parts. The two ship's ventilators are beautifully made brass ones which I acquired cheaply as part of a small collection of miscellaneous model ship fittings, many of which have proved very useful for all sorts of landlubberly purposes around Craig. Some of the brass stanchions, for example, have made very nice locomotive handrail knobs.

Mr. Stevenson, the manager of Peter Allan's Processing Plant lives in a detached modern villa on the lower slopes of Craighill. The most interesting thing about him from our point of view is the fact that he is a model railway enthusiast, and he has laid down a 7½ in gauge oval of track in his front garden. Here he tests the live-steamers which he will later display on the much more extensive track owned by the Craigshire Model Railway Club which meets every Tuesday in the old shed next to the Church Hall on the outskirts of the town. Until just recently the parish minister was the Rev. W. G. Evans who happened to be yet another railway enthusiast—and that's how the Club got the old shed! The Rev. has now moved up to Aberdeenshire, but still keeps in touch with his old friends at Craig.

villa made from an Anorma building kit, and notable for the fact that its garden contained an outdoor model railway. Its scale was approximately half a millimetre to the foot ("quintublo"!) Needless to say, there was no electric motor in the diminutive locomotive, but it nevertheless managed to haul its two coaches at a fair lick around its oval of track and really looked most impressive doing so. Indeed, there were several occasions when visitors to Craigshire there obviously much more intrigued by this garden railway than by the whole of the rest of the C.M.R.—a fact which probably pointed a moral somewhere—but which was nevertheless somewhat galling to my own pride—especially since the whole thing was nothing more than a small clockwork toy which I picked up one Christmas for the quite modest

sum of 5/6d. At the time there were quite a number of these ultra-miniature railways in the toy shops, but I haven't seen one around for quite some time now.

Basically, it consisted of a clockwork motor mounted inside a totally enclosed box. The motor drove a large pulley wheel and this, in its turn, drove another similar pulley via a long elastic band. Tags on this band engaged pins which projected down from the little locomotive and its coaches, and the "track" upon which the train ran thus consisted of a continuous slot matching up with the elastic band underneath. The two sides of the slot were held in position by means of a large tunnel and a foot-bridge. It would, I imagine, be quite possible to build up a fairly complicated track layout utilizing a number of pulleys, and, if it could somehow be arranged to switch from one route to another on a sort of "cable-car" principle, then "quintublo" could become quite a practical proposition—the "table railway" to end all table railways, in fact!

Craig harbour itself consisted of an irregularly shaped piece of pale green "ripple" glass which was obtained as "salvage material" in the days after the War when wood, glass, or any other basic material was obtainable only by official licence, surreptitiously under-the-counter, or, as in this case, as "salvage

Tramcar No. 3 in the suburbs near Craighill.

material" which few people in their right minds were expected to want anyway. The timber for the layout baseboards also came from this source—the wood being knotted, or warped, or in some other way less than perfect. It is still in use, of course, and seems much better stuff than most of the wood available nowadays.

The buildings at the back of the harbour were a most miscellaneous collection. Some were purely imaginary, a couple were from John H. Ahern plans, one or two were from kits, and the rest were based upon interesting buildings in various parts of Scotland. There was, for example, a group of three pleasantly proportioned houses from Haddington, and a model of some fishermen's cottages from Kirkcaldy. These stood next to another interesting block owned by the National Trust for Scotland and the whole formed a very picturesque group of buildings. Now the cottages have been demolished and half the effect of the National Trust-owned houses has been lost. Thus Scotland preserves its heritage. However, I am not the only person who found the group interesting enough to model, and I can recollect seeing another (and better) model illustrated a few years ago in, I think, the "Model Railway News." So at least the buildings have not vanished without trace.

All these Harbour Street buildings were frontages only, since there seemed no point in modelling backs which would never be seen. However, they were not "semi-flats" of a mere one or two inches depth, but full width buildings. This was perhaps a little bit wasteful of space, but it meant that a natural looking photograph could be taken of the street from any angle. The standard of modelling on some of the buildings was not very high, since the idea in the early days was to get together a row of background houses as quickly as possible in an attempt to give some feeling of completeness to a layout which was taking too many years to build. Of course, I intended to replace them as soon as possible with much better buildings, but the time in which to do this never seemed to become available and the original buildings survived intact right up until a few years ago. They were, indeed, something like the immediate post-war "pre-fabs" which were intended to last a mere ten or twelve years but which, in some places, are actually still with us.

The harbour itself was never fully completed at the far end and this is why there are so few photographs extant of this part of Craig. In the harbour, there was a handful of rowing boats and small pleasure

Out in the country: A pleasant shot of "Alistair" passing through "Ormistone" en route for Craig.

craft, a plastic tugboat (from a Revell kit, I think) and an almost completed model of one of the sailing brigantines which used to ply up and down the east coast of Britain throughout the nineteenth and well into the present century. I myself last saw one of them about twenty years ago at Newhaven harbour near Edinburgh, and have kicked myself ever since for not rushing back the next day armed with camera and tape-measure. My own model—the "Condor"—was based upon a water-line model on display in the Royal Scottish Museum, Edinburgh, and upon photographs of similar ships in magazines and books. At the present moment all these ships are in dry-dock in the boxroom, since Craig Harbour has been filled in. They are not forgotten, however, and are due for a new lease of life when the third phase of Craigshire's history gets under way since this envisages the harbour's return.

The original station buildings at Craig were based upon one of the plans which were obtainable to supplement the drawings at the back of John H. Ahern's book on "Miniature Building Construction." The station portrayed did not represent any particular building, but it was very representative of the thousand and one unpretentious little stations which used to be such a familiar part of the railway scene. The

buildings at Craig made use of Merco "new brick" and "random grey tile" building papers, and looked most effective in spite of the fact that these papers are almost more to scale for 7 mm than for 4 mm scale modelling. However, I have always been rather fond of this range of building papers and still make considerable use of them. After all, the human eye is accommodating only up to a certain point, and it is a fact that the pattern of dead scale brickwork in 4 mm scale tends to be lost unless examined at very close quarters, so that one could argue that there is some justification for using larger than scale bricks simply in order to get an effect of brickwork which would otherwise be lost. Similarly the amount of actual relief afforded by some modern grey-tiled roofs is very small, and in 4 mm scale is probaby most truthfully rendered by a sheet of practically flat tile-paper. This, however, does not satisfy anyone striving after super-detail, and many modellers nowadays model roofs with tiling "strips" laid one on top of the other so as to give enhanced relief. This looks very effective, and is the method I used myself when I came to build a second station building at Craig.

This new station building was a model of that at Polton, a few miles south of Edinburgh. Polton is a place which has long intrigued me. It lies deep in the valley of the river Esk and seems remarkably

Beyond Ormistone the C.M.R. had quite a broad river to cross, and it did so by means of the somewhat primitive timber bridge illustrated here.

remote from the bustling world so close above it. The poet De Quincy lived there, and the neighbourhood has associations with Dryden and Drummond of Hawthornden. A couple of centuries ago the area was renowned for its beauty, but coal-mining, paper-making and suburban sprawl and squalor have all taken their toll. Mind you, it was the paper mills which gave Polton its life in recent years, and now that they have closed down the place has virtually ceased to exist. Railway station, corner shop, post office, and most of the workers' cottages have all been demolished, and it is hard standing there today to visualize the neat little place which I first saw in the late nineteen-forties.

As it was then, Polton had obvious virtues from a modelling point of view, and the station layout was a remarkably compact example of a small branch-line terminus. The station building was a very typical North British Railway structure of the sort which the Company erected all over the Lothians, and I prepared a plan of it which was published in the "Railway Modeller" as long ago as February 1952. By the time I came to construct a model from the plan the building was no more, but I like to think that my model is a fairly faithful reproduction of the original.

I used American "North-Eastern" scribed basswood for the wood-panelled frontage, while the

N.B.-type valances around the projecting canopy were made from thin card, with the planking divisions ruled on with pencil and the small circular holes pricked out with a pin. I really took my time over this model because I wanted a model worthy of the memory of my only really worth-while footplate run on a standard-gauge steam locomotive. This took place long after Polton station had been closed to passenger traffic, but it was still used by the occasional goods train, and one day when I had a free morning I went down to take some photographs and there was an old N.B. "S"-class 0-6-0 pottering about with a few wagons and vans. I got talking to the driver and eventually he said, "Well, we're away now. Hop on, and I'll take you as far as Hardengreen Junction." So we rattled off past the paper mills, across the magnificent viaduct just outside Lasswade, through the tunnel (fortunately we were travelling tender-first), past the junction with the line to Peebles, and finally we rolled to a halt at Hardengreen just outside Eskbank—only three miles in all—but three miles never to be forgotten!

It is sad that little places such as Polton have to go. For decades they seem safe and secure, with a solid air of permanency about them, and then before one

STATION BUILDING AT POLTON (N.B.R.)

FEET.

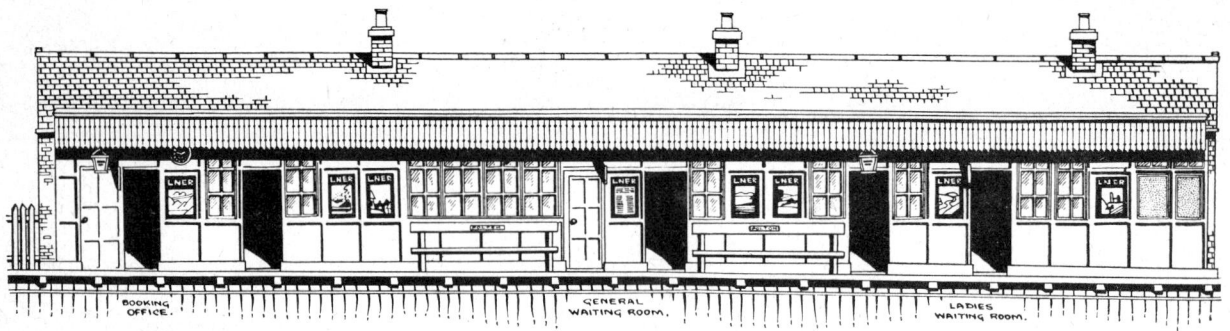

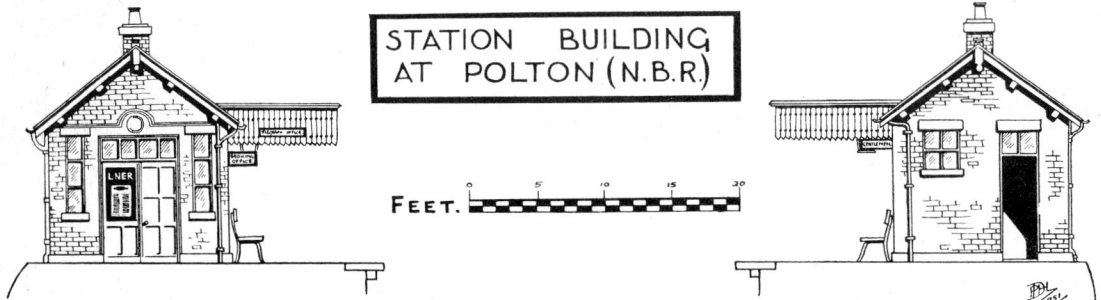

If you go down the steep, winding road from Loanhead into the valley of the River North Esk in Midlothian, you will come to the remains of the once pleasant little village of Polton. It is still possible to work out where the railway station was, but if you want to see what the actual building looked like you will have to come to Craig where the N.B.R. erected an absolutely identical structure. This is not such a remarkable coincidence as it might seem, for Polton station was a very typical N.B. station building.

realizes what is happening they have been caught up by the wind of change and are either swept away or emerge transformed. So it was at Craig! All the features which I have been describing became pretty well known to regular readers of the "Railway Modeller" during the nineteen-fifties, and when I eventually began to transform what had been a purely narrow-gauge layout into a combined standard and narrow-gauge layout, quite a number of these readers were duly horrified. In fact, the way in which Craigshire had managed to acquire a life of its own did have its slightly alarming side, and on more than one occasion I was embarrassed by visitors to the layout who had evidently been "swotting up" on my articles, and who possessed an encyclopaedic knowledge of the C.M.R.'s history which seemed far greater than my own. When it became quite evident that the C.M.R. was going to have to share Craig with an ever increasing amount of standard-gauge track, one of my regular correspondents wrote to tell me that he feared the worst, and that he proposed

to form a "Craig and Mertonford Railway Preservation Society." To scotch rumours that the narrow-gauge might be abandoned altogether the "Railway Modeller" published a picture on one of its covers of the C.M.R.'s 2-4-0, "Agnes", complete with the caption, "This branch not to close!"

I must admit that this was an awkward time at Craig. I was really trying to squeeze too much into my available space, and was not prepared to face up to the fact that what was needed was a completely redesigned layout. Instead I tinkered about, trying first one scheme and then another in the attempt to blend the standard-gauge more happily with the narrow-gauge. Several "outrages" were committed during this period, and about these it may be best to say nothing. After all, most of them were very short-lived, and since they never found their way into the pages of the "Railway Modeller" I can conveniently pretend that they never happened. In the end, circumstances did conspire to force a complete rebuild of the layout upon me, but before that happened I had taken the somewhat momentous decision to turn back the clock at Craig from the present to the Edwardian era. This in itself was almost the same as making a new start, and, ironically enough, a fairly satisfactory blend of the narrow and standard gauges actually was achieved just before the whole lot had to be swept away.

6   Putting back the clock

Salvation began to come with the decision to turn back the clock to pre-Grouping days. Here Craig's new Edwardian inhabitants parade in all their finery on Craig Station platform by the old buildings.

The idea of re-modelling Craig as it might have been about the turn of the century was one that had been growing upon me for some time. Perhaps it stemmed from a certain disenchantment with the mid-twentieth century; perhaps merely from a growing reluctance to paint my new and painstakingly built standard-gauge locomotives the normal British Railways livery of mud brown and dirt grey! Whatever the reasons, I began to see more and more attractions and advantages in the idea of a layout set round about the year 1912—not 1912 definitely—but just "some time" vaguely before the outbreak of the First World War.

I am fully aware that this was not a golden age for everybody, and that there was, in fact, a great deal of poverty and misery underneath the surface show and glitter. And yet, when all is said and done, it is quite apparent that for very many elderly people the age does appear as a kind of high watermark in European civilization, and even among those who were poor and underprivileged there is often regret for the passing of some of the virtues and ways of life of the time. It was, after all, a much quieter, more leisurely, and less frightening age than ours. Above all it was

a confident age—an age secure in the knowledge that scientific progress was going to go on making the world a better place for everyone. Only in the writings of that strange man, Mr. H. G. Wells, was there any foreboding that Science might just possibly have opened a Pandora's box which could threaten the whole future of Mankind.

By 1912 there were, of course, faint rumblings on the horizon, but even the prospect of a vast European conflict was not quite the daunting thing it seems to us in retrospect. There were strikes, there was trouble in Ireland, but Britain had survived the test of the Boer War, and still ruled an Empire upon which the sun never set. The pageantry of the previous year's Delhi Durbar had roused patriotic echoes in the hearts of peers and costermongers alike. It was still a familiar world. Errand boys whistled as they rode their bicycles through the streets, and the jingle of harness and the clip-clop of horses hooves still predominated over the malodorous throbbing of the new-fangled motor cars. The Sherlock Holmes stories were appearing in the "Strand" magazine. Mr. George Bernard Shaw was busy writing "Pygmalion." The streets were lit by gaslight, hansom cabs plied

41

The only real difference between this scene and that on p. 31 is that time has somehow slipped a cog and we are back in the days of hansom cabs, gaslight and pre-Grouping railways. Here North British Railway 4-4-0 "Kettledrummle" hauls a train of East Coast Joint Stock six-wheelers into Craig station, while a "C" class 0-6-0 loco. waits on the harbour siding. Actually, the change-over to pre-Grouping days was rather sudden and there are at least two anachronisms in the picture. No prizes for spotting them!

for hire, and—of course—it was the hey-day of the railways!

The early pioneering days were over, and now there were over one hundred different railway companies each with its own distinctive ways and its own distinctive locomotive and coach liveries. Travel across Britain, and you would find green locomotives and red locomotives, blue locomotives, brown locomotives, and even yellow locomotives! And what a variety of different types there were, and what a plenitude of different initials to juggle with: G.N.R., G.W.R., L.N.W.R., G.C.R., L.B. and S.C.R.—there was simply no end to them!

And, remember, those were the days when locomotives were not just cleaned, but cleaned until they shone and sparkled!

Craigshire, of course, was in the territory of the North British and the North Eastern Railway companies, so that the decision to "go pre-Grouping" involved me in much interesting research into the history and practices of those companies. However, to explain away the odd-looking locos, coaches or equipment which might appear at Craig, I evolved the story that the line from Dunbar to Craig had originally been built by the Craigshire Northern Railway Company, a concern which soon went bankrupt and was bought up by the N.B.R. The Craigshire Northern indulged in such things as stretches of track laid with flat-bottom rail and in signals with plain wooden posts, and these survived for many years after the North British had taken over.

Another C.N.R. survival at Craig was the gallows type turntable. A turntable of some sort became necessary at Craig as soon as I introduced tender locomotives to the layout, and I chose to model an American-style gallows turntable largely because of the ease with which the current collection problem could be solved by means of an overhead wire to the centre of the gallows—an Edward Beal idea, this. The turntable was a fraction over ten inches long and was designed to be just capable of taking a model of an N.B. Atlantic locomotive and tender. It was

N.B.R. "A" class 0-6-2T No. 42 shunting goods wagons at Craig Harbour, while N.E.R. 4-4-0 No. 621 runs light into Craig station.

powered from underneath the baseboard by a large 6-volt Japanese electric motor and a collection of Meccano gears and other bits and pieces ("Heath-Robinsonish" was not the word for it!") However, the result of all the gearing was a nice, slowly revolving turntable, and this was rather important because there were no automatic gadgets to stop the motor when the tracks were lined up. I had to judge things by eye and switch off the motor at precisely the right moment. This probably sounds more fearsome than it really was, since I found, after a little practice, that I could manage to stop the turntable in the correct

Another view of Craig station with N.B.R. No. 425, "Kettledrummle", on the turntable. This was electrically operated from underneath the baseboard by a small 6-volt Japanese electric motor and Meccano reduction gearing. Just in front of the turntable there is a small crane-operated coaling stage, and in the immediate foreground half a dozen off-duty railwaymen are indulging in a game of pitch-and-toss.

position nine times out of ten. On the tenth occasion a little juggling to and fro would soon get things right.

Surprisingly little needed to be done at Craig in order to make the switch back to pre-Grouping days. There were no "modern" buildings on the layout anyway, and the station building had already been converted to a North British prtootype. The Craig and District Electric Traction Company tramway was beautifully in period, and it was an easy matter to sweep all motor vehicles from the streets and replace them with horse-drawn vehicles. Quite a bit of fun was had re-dressing the local citizenry in period costume, and there is no doubt that the women's long dresses and large hats did quite a bit to create the right atmosphere. Most of the figures used were of the ordinary commercial variety, and these were altered with the aid of plastic wood, paper, glue, and any other media which seemed appropriate. On the whole, it turned out to be a fairly quick job to alter the shapes; it was the painting of the finished figures that took all the time. Mind you, I think it was time well spent, and it was quite fascinating doing it—even if I did feel at the end of the day that I ought perhaps to have been using a watchmaker's eyeglass.

The Hornby Dublo footbridge was eventually replaced by a home-made lattice footbridge which fitted much better into the pre-Grouping atmosphere. It was made from fine wire mesh, bullhead rail, a great deal of solder, and a certain amount of cursing and swearing. Nowadays there are some fine brass stampings and even complete bridge kits which would enable me to produce a much better job in a fraction of the time, but I doubt if the sense of achievement would be as great as that which I experienced when this effort, with all its faults, first went into service, enabling passengers to cross in style.

However, it was the arrival of genuine pre-Grouping railway equipment at Craig which really completed the Edwardian picture. For the opening ceremony we had a model of N.B.R. "Scott" class 4-4-0 "Kettledrummle", over which I had shed blood, sweat and tears for the previous five months, and also a model of a "C" class 0-6-0 which went together very much more quickly. Indeed, quite a number of liberties were taken in its construction, and it was decided that these had better be explained

Right: Aerial view of Craig station, showing a further extension of the standard-gauge tracks at the expense of the C.M.R. However, as though to compensate for its losses at Craig, the narrow-gauge line now circumnavigated the room. The curved track in the left foreground led to a lift-out bridge which linked Craig to Glenmuir and permitted continuous running when desired.

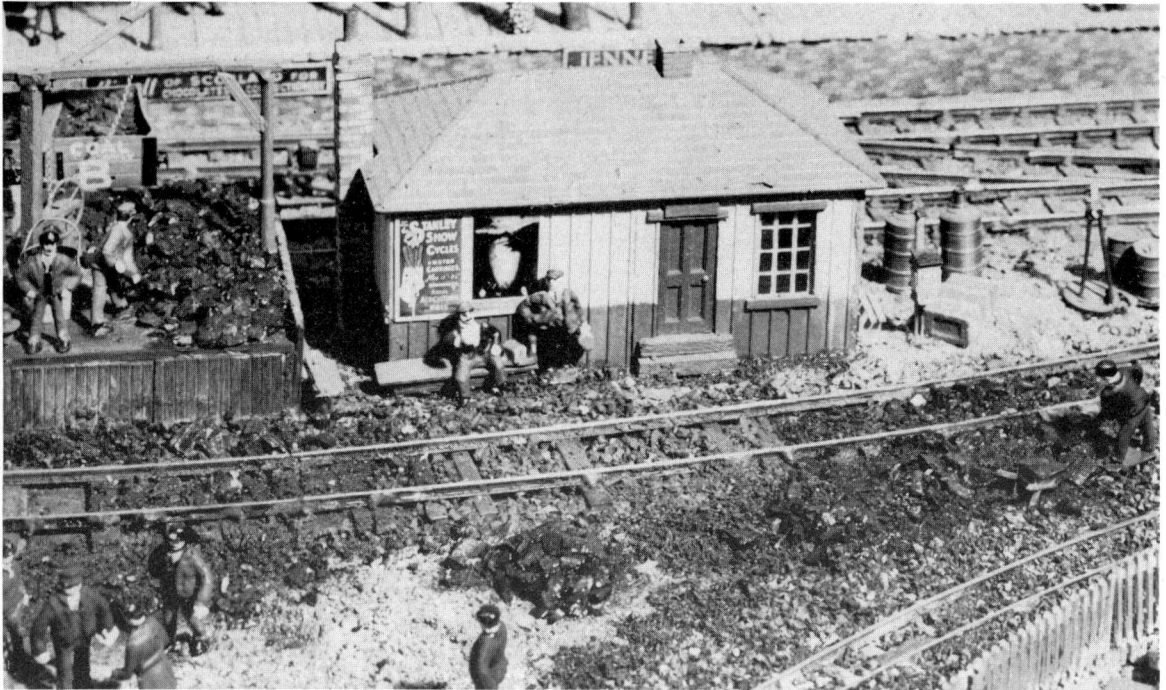

N.B.R. style locomen's hut, complete with a couple of period posters and two off-duty locomen having a chat and a cuppa. At the spot where Spud Tamson is shovelling away the cinders there were a couple of pea bulbs embedded in the ground underneath the cinders and underneath a layer of red cellophane. A touch on the appropriate switch on the control panel would make the cinders glow most realistically.

away by the fiction that the loco originally came from the Craigshire Northern Railway. There was a considerable amount of ex-C.N.R. equipment among the rolling stock as well, and it was only very gradually that a few genuine N.B. wagons and a couple of brake vans were built and added to the stock. However, about a dozen "standard" planked wagons of various origins (Triang, Hornby Dublo, Peco, K.'s etc.) were repainted in Edinburgh district private owners' liveries and these were most effective. The passenger stock consisted of five Exley six-wheelers which looked something like East Coast Joint Stock coaches, and so were painted accordingly. Later these were followed by three K.'s L.B. & S.C. four-wheelers, which required very little adaptation to make them resemble the coaches illustrated on page 38 of George Dow's little booklet upon "The First Railway Across the Border."* Triang's G.W.R. clerestory coaches proved also to be as near to certain North Eastern Railway coach designs as to make no difference, and the final grandiose touch was provided by a train of seven Hornby Dublo Pullman coaches,

* The First Railway Across the Border. By George Dow, A.M.Inst.T. Issued by the London & North Eastern Railway to commemorate the opening of the North British Railway one hundred years ago. Edin., pr. 1946.

titivated up slightly and renamed where necessary. These never had much scope on the original layout, and had to await the day when they could be marshalled behind our N.B.R. Atlantic, "Hazeldean" and let loose upon the continuous-run which was built into the second layout.

In earlier days I had always tended to frown upon the continuous-run as an un-railwaylike feature, reminiscent of toy-train days, but as the years passed, I became more and more aware of the advantages it could offer as a sort of testing ground, and as an easy means of letting trains have their head once in a while. The first continuous run actually appeared before the layout had to be rebuilt, and as a glance at the accompanying plan shows, it was the narrow-gauge C.M.R. which first succeeded in circumnavigating the railway room. Mind you, this happened almost accidentally. Once the line had reached Glenmuir, there was only the width of the door separating it from Craig itself, so what more

The narrow-gauge station building at Craig.

natural than the provision of a removable bridge to enable the two to be linked up? The layout was still operated on a point-to-point basis, but it was now possible to indulge in continuous running when I felt like it, and I have to admit that I found it rather fun.

At this time also, Craig station was properly rebuilt as a combined standard and narrow-gauge station, and a quite impressive works yard blossomed forth at the side of Craig locomotive shed. In some ways this was an extension of the scrap heap at the back of the shed; it was never properly wired into the rest of the system and remained as a scenic adjunct, useful for storing locomotives and other vehicles awaiting attention. There was a locomotive-hoist based upon a design in one of Edward Beal's books, a turntable, and some rather nice works buildings. The locomotive shed itself dated from the very early days of the layout and was an imposingly large structure for such a minor railway as the Craig and Mertonford. This is because it actually anteceded the C.M.R. It was one of the first models I ever built, and was intended for an ordinary standard gauge layout. It was fully detailed inside, and I cannot

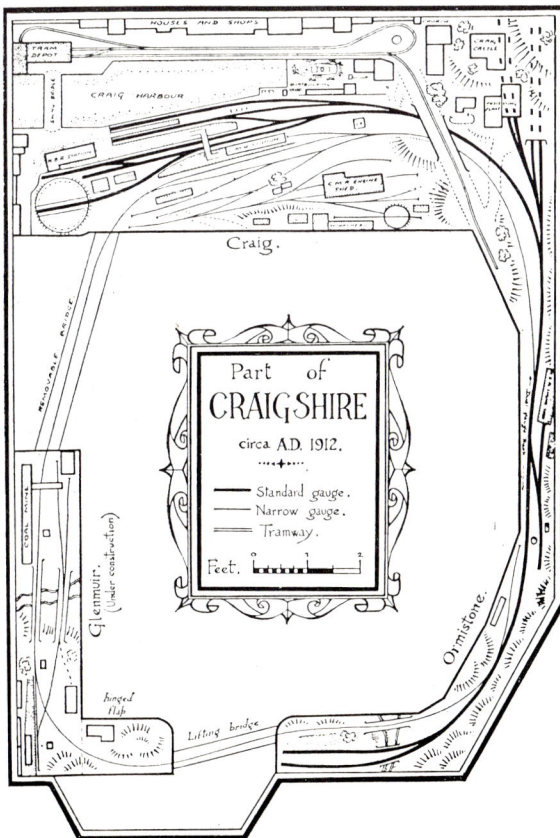

Part of CRAIGSHIRE

circa A.D. 1912.

Standard gauge.
Narrow gauge.
Tramway.

Feet.

N.B.R. "Jubilee" wagon at Craig. This is the spot where locos. dump their ashes on the line, and poor old Spud Tamson, whom you see on the right there, has to shovel them up and cart them away when the deposit grows too large.

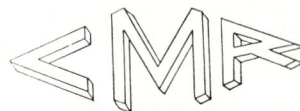

(GOLD LETTERS, WITH RED SHADING.)

imagine why I never took any photographs of the interior. The reader will just have to take my word for it that it was something really rather special.

Over the years the Craig and Mertonford acquired a most remarkable collection of rolling stock—the result, no doubt, of Lord Craig's various attempts to economize by purchasing things second-hand, or rebuilding old stock to new requirements. For a long time the only two decent passenger coaches on the system were two American-style bogie coaches. These were built from Kemtron photo-engraved sides and lost-wax castings, and were adaptations of Denver and Rio Grande Western prototypes. The original C.M.R. livery for these coaches consisted of white upper panels, maroon lower panels, and a rather ornate heraldic crest. This was later changed in order to provide more of a contrast with the maroon of the standard-gauge N.B. coaches, and the maroon and white of the tramcars. The first new livery adopted was somewhat akin to the pre-Second World War L.N.E.R. tourist livery, and is illustrated in the accompanying diagram. The ornate crest was also replaced by a more easily painted monogram. Why this had to be changed yet again I don't really know. I think Lord Craig must have been paying some visits to Wales, because only a little while afterwards the coaches were again repainted, this time with cream upper panels and chocolate brown lower panels—all very reminiscent of the Great Western Railway. This is still the official livery at the time of writing—the fact that three of our new coaches are green, one is still maroon, and only two are cream and chocolate is just one of those things that one comes to expect in Craigshire.

All the original C.M.R. stock was built to a scale of 4.5 mm to the foot rather than 4 mm to the foot. This was due to the fact that the great difficulty in the early days was that of getting electric motors into the small locomotives. None of the currently available "N" gauge motors existed, and it was a case of either building one's own motors, or else building things just that little bit larger than they ought to be. With the facilities and skills available at Craig Workshops there was really no choice! Now "N" gauge equipment has become available, and it is even possible to purchase ready-to-run 3.5 mm scale narrow-gauge equipment. There is thus no longer any excuse for overscale coaches and wagons on the C.M.R., and much of the old stock has now been retired, including the two faithful Kemtron bogie coaches. However, I am very loath to see these vanish altogether, and hope to be able to rebuild them to reduced dimensions at some time in the not too far distant future.

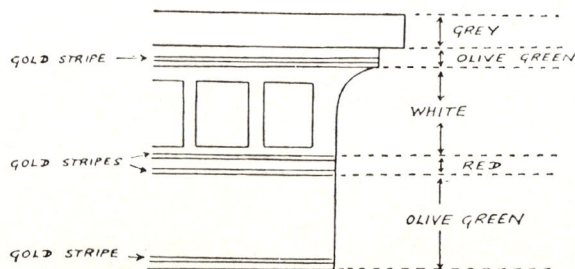

7 The second Craigshire

Even while I was busy putting back the clock at Craig, I was conscious that there was a Damocles sword suspended above the layout, and I knew that everything would soon have to be closed down and dismantled. Mind you, the closure was none of my seeking—other, and higher, authorities were involved! I had just finished writing an article for the "Railway Modeller" about the pre-Grouping developments when I became aware of a voice speaking to me. It turned out to be the Voice of Doom!

"This room", said the Voice of Doom, "has got to be redecorated."

"But this room," said I, "houses the Craig and Mertonford Light Railway—not to mention the Craigshire branch of the North British Railway, and the Craig and District Electric Traction Company tramway system."

"It also happens to be your bedroom," said the Voice of Doom, "and it's ten years since it was decorated."

"Perhaps," I said, "I could myself paint the walls—from the ceiling down as far as the top of the layout—and then from the bottom of the layout to the floor."

"! ! ! ! ! ! ! !" said the Voice of Doom.

So, in 1961, the breakers moved in, salvaging what could be salvaged and ruthlessly destroying everything else. Soon it was as though Craig and the C.M.R. had never existed. Mind you, the dismantling was something which I had envisaged away back in 1949 or thereabouts when work on the layout first

There is now a tunnel under Craighill, and here N.B.R. 4-4-2 Atlantic locomotive "Hazeldean" storms out of the entrance at the head of the mid-day Craigshire Pullman. This photograph gives a fine view of the unusually-shaped tunnel entrance. Some people have expressed doubts about the stability of such a shape—but there it is, with the date of building (1897) plain for all to see—so it has evidently stood the test of time for at least fifteen years!

There are quite a few people watching the trains go by from the path which passes behind the tunnel entrance, thus proving that "train spotting" is no new thing. Indeed, we all know that it was the ambition of all right-minded Edwardian schoolboys to become engine drivers.

Incidentally, just outside the tunnel there is a rail joint with a purposely large gap in it, so that trains emerging from the tunnel do so with a beautiful clickety-click, clickety-click, clickety-click. I have discovered that this one large gap in each running rail is all that is required to achieve the effect.

began, and the original idea had been that everything was to be of a semi-portable nature. Alas for good intentions! As the years rolled on, and alterations and fresh additions were made, it had become only too easy to lay new track across the joints of what were supposed to be sections, to carry the wiring round the layout in unbroken lengths, and even to build scenery on top of the screws which held the various parts together. In short, when it came to putting the portability of the layout actually to the test it proved to be just about as portable as a brontosaurus. The position of those screws which I mentioned a moment ago was a secret known only to the gods, and to find them again much scenery had to be ruthlessly torn up, Rails and wiring had to be sawn through, and trees and buildings uprooted. By the time I had finished it was pretty obvious that Craigshire was going to take a lot of putting together again.

Well, you can guess what happened next, can't you? I mean to say, any modeller worth his salt would, at this stage, immediately investigate the possibility

Craig locomotive depot is a very modest affair. This view was evidently taken at a very slack part of the day. The yard foreman slumbers in a chair propped up against the toolshed, while drivers Jock Armstrong and Angus MacTavish enjoy a "cuppa" and the attentions of a passing dog nosing around for titbits. Jock's bicycle (wire bent to shape and soldered) leans against the wall of the staff hut. The locos. on shed are all N.B. types—the 0-6-0 class "C" goods loco., the 4-4-2 "Yorkie" No. 26, and the 4-4-0 "Scott" class passenger locomotive "Kettledrummle" of which only the tender is visible.

As you can see, the pointwork is all operated by hand levers. On the first layout most of the points were operated by solenoid motors from the control panel, and the hand levers on the second layout were originally fitted as yet another "temporary" measure. However, after a little experience of hand operation I discovered that, far from offending my aesthetic sensibilities, it actually seemed more satisfying to move the lever by the side of the actual point.

of building a new layout—a much better layout, of course—the layout, in fact, which he should have built in the first place, but which, somehow or other, just failed to materialize! So while the painters and the carpenters and the plasterers were getting on with the redecorating, I was busy at the drawing board evolving new and better Craigshires.

Three resolutions were made at the very beginning.

Firstly, the new layout would have a continuous run as an integral part of either the standard or the narrow gauge system.

Secondly, curves on the standard gauge would have a minimum radius of 3 ft (91 cm) and curves on the narrow-gauge a minimum radius of 2 ft (61 cm).

Thirdly, the layout would be built in self-contained sections, each no bigger than about 3 ft by 18 in (91 cm by 46 cm).

Right: Craig castle and the station approaches on the second layout. The second Craig is certainly far more urban in character than was the first, and this might be considered a little odd in view of the fact that it is supposed to precede it in time by some fifty years. However, this simply reflects the changing fortunes of Craigshire as a whole, and, in particular, the decline of the once all-important shale mining industry. In Edwardian times, moreover, most people had their holidays in Britain rather than abroad, and Craig was a popular resort for people in Edinburgh who wanted a Highland holiday more or less on their own doorstep, or for people in Northumberland who wished to savour something of the "real Scotland" but who could not afford to travel all the way to Speyside or Lochaber. Nowadays people fly to Europe or even further afield, neglecting the beauties on their own doorstep. It is amazing, indeed, how many people have never even heard of Craigshire! Come to think of it, maybe this is not altogether a bad thing. If the area were better known it might be "developed", and then we might get a motorway slicing through the Craigshire hills.

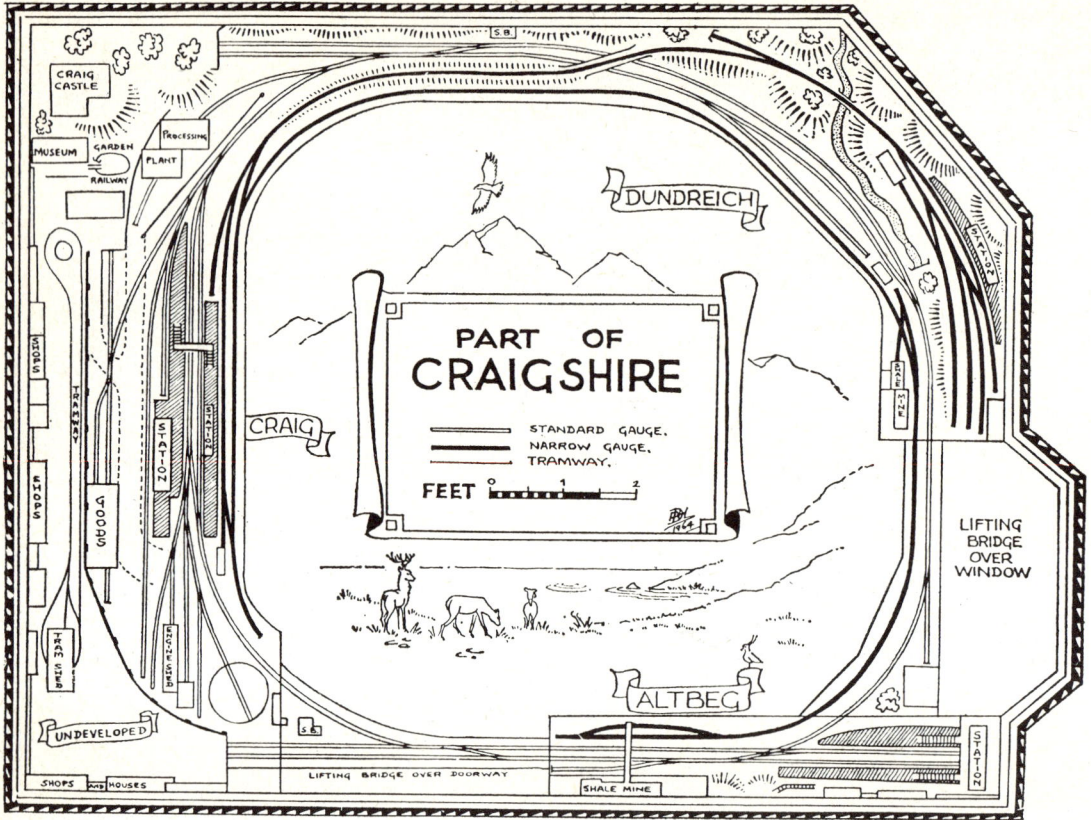

PART OF CRAIGSHIRE

STANDARD GAUGE.
NARROW GAUGE.
TRAMWAY.

FEET 0 1 2

These are all things which have been recommended time and time again by the long established experts, but my own experience seems to prove that few people pay any attention to them until, like me, they learn their value by bitter experience.

Mind you, even now, the first resolution is still a little controversial in my own mind. I have already mentioned how the C.M.R. first came to circumnavigate the railway room, and it was this which won me round to the idea of a continuous run. It is true that the spectacle of trains chasing their own tails round and round a room does pall after a time, but then, unless one has a very long length of run to operate, it can also become a trifle tedious just shuttling back and forth between point A and point B—no matter how much shunting about of locomotives and stock there may be at each end. Indeed, the desire to be able to "pull out all the stops" and just "let 'em rip" becomes something of an obsession after a time. So perhaps the ideal would be the layout which could be operated on a point-to-point basis but which also provided the opportunity for contin-

uous running when desired. In the case of Craigshire the final result was something of a compromise, with a continuous run for the standard gauge and point-to-point operation on the narrow-gauge C.M.R.

The second resolution brooks little argument—the wider the radius of the curve the better. It looks more realistic, it helps to prevent buffer locking, and it prevents that ugly overhang which one gets at the front of some model locomotives when they are forced

Craig station is a model of Polton station, now demolished. The top photograph on the facing page gives quite a clear view of the typical N.B. wood-panelled frontage and distinctive valancing. The lower view shows the equally characteristic projecting canopy. Behind the station is the goods shed and an assortment of wagons, including one from the far south of England. The photograph shows the wagons fitted with Triang "TT" gauge couplers, but these have now all been replaced by ordinary prototypical three-link couplings. I have an uncoupling device consisting of a pencil torch with hook attached, and find that coupling and uncoupling with this is much more fun than it ever was with automatic couplers. Besides, it is fascinating to watch a train getting under way in the correct manner, wagon by wagon, instead of all in one go—or else slowly backing up a train with a realistic clattering of buffers.

*One of the main differences between the old and the new
layouts lies in the fact that the background main street has
now been raised about three inches above the level of the
station. This is necessary because the concealed storage
sidings lie underneath, but the general effect is quite good. It
has necessitated a steep road near Craighill, descending
from street level to the station, and, as can be seen in the
photograph, I originally had marching down this a version
of the Airfix Guards band and colour party. However, my
lack of knowledge about military bands landed me in a little
bit of trouble. I first referred to the troops in an article in
the "Railway Modeller" as a detachment of the Scots
Guards on a recruiting campaign to Craig. This wasn't too
bad; but in a later article I slipped up and described them
instead as a detachment of the Craigshire Yeomanry. This
was too much for my military readers, one of whom—N. B.
Collins—wrote politely to the correspondence columns to
point out that the uniforms were not those of a yeomanry
regiment and that the composition of the band was horribly
wrong.*

to negotiate too sharp a curve. However, I must admit
that in designing the new Craigshire I was eventually
forced to incorporate one curve of 2 ft 6 in (76 cm)
on the main line and a couple of 2 ft (61 cm) radius
turnouts in the goods yard—but at least I did *try*
to keep every curve as wide as possible and the result
certainly looked much better than did the sharp
curves on the old layout.

The third resolution—to build in sections—was,
of course, the result of my experience in dismantling
the old layout, and a determined effort was made to
ensure that any subsequent dismantling would not
necessarily mean complete demolition.

As can be seen from the accompanying plan, the
new Craigshire bore a strong resemblance to the old,
but there was one important basic difference. To
a large extent the old layout had "just grown", and
while it had quite a number of picturesque qualities
it was not a good layout from the operational point
of view. Operation on the second layout was very
much more interesting, but I have to admit that in
order to achieve this some of the scenic virtues of
the old Craigshire were lost. Craig itself was still
recognizably Craig, with the castle perched on top
of its hill, and the tramway still running in front of
the same row of background shops and houses, but
the harbour vanished—and somehow Craig just
didn't seem Craig without it. It vanished simply
because I developed a peculiar blank spot in my mind
when it came to considering possible ways of com-
bining it with the requirements of the new layout.
I was quite unable to think of a pictorially satisfactory
way of carrying the railway tracks past the harbour
entrance, and the obvious solution did not dawn upon
me until years later.

Ormistone and Glenmuir, as such, also vanished.
They developed upon such completely new lines that
it seemed best to rechristen them. Ormistone became
Dundreich (named after a favourite Peebles-shire
hill) and Glenmuir, which had been more or less in
the wilds, now became the little village of Altbeg. In
actual fact, Altbeg was simply built on top of Glenmuir. It was necessary to raise the level a bit, and
since there seemed little prospect of salvaging much
of the track at Glenmuir I decided simply to lay a
convenient sheet of plywood on top of the existing

Right: General view of Dundreich, which is now the headquarters of the C.M.R. Here a short train has just arrived at the station—two small four-wheel coaches hauled by the Company's only passenger-carrying railcar—a Hamo tram body on top of a narrow-gauged Romford motor bogie.

There is a notice on the station building telling people not to cross the line, but, as is the case with many narrow-gauge concerns, nobody pays any attention to it, and, as the photograph shows, people disembark on whichever side of the train they see fit. Indeed, Sandy Macdonald has driven his horse and trap right on to the line, so that he will have less distance to carry all the luggage which his niece is sure to have brought with her from the wilds of suburban Hampshire and over the lines of five different railway companies.

On the left, "Roderick" at the head of a short goods train prepares to depart for Craig now that the single-track line is clear.

In the right foreground is an interesting relic of horse tramway days on the C.M.R.—a hand-winch operated stub point—one of Lord Craig's "patents", of course—no frog, no blades, no nothing—but it works!

It is a fine sunny morning in early spring. Every sound carries in the clear country air, and the hiss of gently escaping steam from "Roderick's" cylinders is blended with the plaintive cry of a peewit and the murmur of the West Water in the valley below the station.

Left: Away back in the nineteen-fifties the late John Allen of Monterey, California, aroused a certain amount of envy in the hearts of all aspiring scenic railway modellers when he unveiled Mount Alexander before the gaze of readers of the "Model Railroader."

Mount Alexander rose from the floor to the level of his Gorre and Daphetid Railroad, and then towered high above it. I longed to be able to erect something similar in Craigshire, but the best I was able to manage was a mere two-and-a-half feet (approx. 75 cm) from baseboard level to the top of Craig Castle. However, at Dundreich I have now at least attempted the illusion of mountain scenery, and in the quite inadequate space of some six inches (15 cm) between track and walls I have raised some cork bark and plaster cliffs rising for about a foot up to a painted backdrop which merges into the colour of the actual wall.

Dundreich station building consists of little more than the bare essentials—a booking office with a room marked "private" for the staff, a ladies waiting room, and a central open area with seats for shelter from the rain. In the sidings, "Duncan" potters about.

track and start afresh. It was only after the new track was actually laid that I realized that the track pins might have penetrated to the old rails underneath and somehow caused a series of mysterious short circuits.

N.E.R. 4-4-0 No. 1321 with a local train to Berwick passes Dundreich shed and workshops. Up on the C.M.R. tracks there is a narrow-gauge loco. of which we have no trace at all on the Company books! Indeed, I cannot even remember building her and have no idea where she went. Seeing her here in this photograph is really rather frightening ... obviously the C.M.R. has now been in existence long enough to acquire its own personal ghosts!

However, all was well—and now it comes as something of a shock when I periodically remember what an archaeologist digging down at Altbeg would uncover.

One thing which rather surprises me when I look back at it is the decision I took to make the standard gauge line double track rather than single track. I really much prefer a single track meandering through the countryside, but in the space available for Craigshire (with a bed in the middle of the room) I was more or less forced to lay the track in straight lengths along the walls and curved round the corners. Since it had to be laid neatly like this, I felt that it might as well be as neat as possible and become a double track main line. This really took up very little more

width than a single track and gave me the added pleasure of being able to run two trains at once and watch them passing each other. It also enabled me to keep my main-line Pullman express on one of the concealed sidings and let it loose once in a while. It may never actually have called at Craig station, but the sight of N.B.R. "Hazeldean" at the head of the seven coach train certainly added something to the Craigshire scene.

This all tended, of course, to push the narrow gauge somewhat into the background, and in order to give added scope to the C.M.R. I did for a time single the standard gauge line between Dundreich and Altbeg so that what had originally been just a narrow gauge siding at Craig could be promoted into a new running track extending all the way to

Dundreich engine shed and the new C.M.R. workshops are maybe not so extensive or impressive as the old ones at Craig, but at least they have a more picturesque setting. At the back of the engine shed Angus McPhwat has already begun to accumulate his usual pile of rubbish, and this has even begun to spill over the fence and down the slope to the West Water. Could that possibly be Angus himself hammering at something just in front of that discarded hopper?

the shale mine at Altbeg. This is the scheme which is actually illustrated on the plan. Strangely enough, it turned out rather unsatisfactorily, largely because the C.M.R. could ill afford to lose its storage sidings. So after about a year I restored the double track standard gauge, and the C.M.R. was cut back to Dundreich again.

"Angus" at the head of some slightly more modern bogie stock, somewhere among the Craigshire Hills.

A busy scene at Dundreich, with a view of Dundreich Hill in the background. Theoretically there is a road behind the railings at the top of the high stone wall, and a flight of steps leads down to the station from the little building perched up there. Dundreich village itself lies somewhere off-stage—a quarter of a mile or so further along the same road.

The entire standard gauge part of the layout was divided into seven sections, each of which could be switched on to either of two available controllers. It was possible to switch the three sections of the up line on to one controller and the three sections of the down line on to the other and thus, as I say, control two trains at once. The system was, I suppose, a kind of simple "cab control". One controller was a Hammant and Morgan "Electran" variable voltage unit, and the other was an ordinary rheostat—a Shenphone C7—fed from an ancient but very reliable Shenphone rectifier. This also supplied current to the narrow gauge C.M.R., which had one controller at Craig station and another at Dundreich, either of which could be switched in or out of circuit as required.

Even although I have a lamentable habit of just running trains whenever I feel like it, I did work out a quite elaborate timetable for the layout (See Appendix 1). This took several hours to work through and never seemed to pall—perhaps because I never had time for all that many operating sessions. An operating session at Craig was something like the icing on top of the cake. My main interest in railway modelling lies in the actual construction of the models and the creation of the landscape picture—but periodically I have to blow the dust off things, clean the tracks, and prove that things really do work!

The best parts of the operating timetable were undoubtedly the goods trains, designated Up Goods or Down Goods according to which way they left Craig station. For these a system of card operation was worked out, based upon an idea described several years ago in the "Model Railroader." Every wagon on the layout had its own individual card, and each card bore a quite arbitrary list of possible destinations, each of which was marked UP (Eastbound) or DOWN (Westbound) according to whether they could best be served by a train travelling in either the up or the down direction. The card for Bruce Lindsay Bros. P.O. wagon is illustrated opposite and gives the general idea. As each journey was completed, so the space on the right of the card was ticked off in pencil, and, when the whole card had been worked through, the pencil ticks were all rubbed out so that one could start again at the beginning.

At each of the destinations there was a little box attached underneath or to the side of the layout, and this held the cards belonging to all the wagons waiting there at any particular time. When a goods train was being sent off from Craig station the procedure was to go through the cards for the wagons at the station and pick out, let us say, all the ones applicable to Up Goods destinations. The station yard then had to be shunted to make up a train from the appropriate

BRUCE LINDSAY BROS COAL WAGON		
DESTINATION		
DUNDREICH	D	✔
CRAIG MARSHALLING YARD		✔
PETER ALLANS	U	✔
CRAIG MARSHALLING YARD		✔
ALTBEG MINE	D	✔
CRAIG MARSHALLING YARD		
ALTBEG STATION	U	
CRAIG MARSHALLING YARD		
ALTBEG YARD	D/U	
CRAIG MARSHALLING YARD		
DUNDREICH	D	
CRAIG MARSHALLING YARD		
ALTBEG MINE	D	
CRAIG MARSHALLING YARD		
PETER ALLANS	U	
CRAIG MARSHALLING YARD		
ALTBEG STATION	U	
CRAIG MARSHALLING YARD		
PETER ALLANS	U	
CRAIG MARSHALLING YARD		
DUNDREICH	D	
CRAIG MARSHALLING YARD		
ALTBEG MINE	D	

D - DOWN   U - UP

"Alistair" can coast easily enough downhill from Dundreich to Craig, but assistance may be needed on the way back, since there are several excursion parties arriving in Craig today, and, in anticipation of heavy traffic, the C.M.R.'s two four-wheeled coaches have been added to the usual rake of three bogie coaches.

wagons, and these had to be arranged in the most convenient order for eventual delivery. The train then set off, and as it went round the layout so the appropriate wagons were set down at the various sidings and any wagons already waiting at the sidings were picked up. Thus, at the end of the journey an entirely new train of wagons was delivered to Craig station goods yard to be re-marshalled for the next goods train.

It might be thought that because there were only three possible destinations for each goods train there would not be very much scope in the system. In actual fact it took a surprisingly long time to run one of these trains and one never knew what would happen next. As I say, the destinations marked on the

59

An early morning line-up of narrow-gauge locomotive power at Dundreich. "Ian", "Duncan", and "Alistair" take on coal and water in preparation for the day's work. In the far background, just in front of the wagon hoist, can be seen the last remains of "Douglas".

cards were purely arbitrary, based merely upon a rough estimate of likely journeys for wagons, and upon repeating the names of the sidings with greater capacity more often than the names of those with little capacity. Nevertheless it would quite often happen when a train was being made up that a sudden plethora of wagons would be required at Altbeg Mine siding perhaps—more even than the siding could hold—and this would mean that an extra train would somehow have to be slipped into the time-table. In all the years of existence of the layout I never actually got to the end of all the possible combinations and permutations concealed by the cards, so that the goods trains were always providing surprises during any operating session. Since there was theoretically only a certain time allowed for the goods trains, and since speedy coupling and un-coupling of the wagons depended upon one's dex-terity with the pencil-torch uncoupling hook, things sometimes became a trifle hectic, and some goods trains completed their journeys at break-neck speed in order to get back to Craig station before the "Pullman" was due to blast out of the tunnel under Craig Hill. True, the goods trains were allowed to potter around the layout while the other trains in the time table were being operated, and it was usually possible to divert them to the other line when a train was due. Nevertheless there would be occasions when the other line would already be occupied, and then, with the timings all haywire, there would be nothing else for it but to hold the express until the line was clear and the Goods had shamefacedly crept back to the station. When this happened we had, so to speak, lost our "battle" with the timetable!

On another part of the hillside Old Andra', the shepherd, has just rescued an orphan lamb and is whistling instructions to Tam, his collie dog, to drive the sheep back from the rather nasty little precipice towards which they are straying. The sheep are mainly Slater's plastic models, but there is also one from a Christmas cracker—the only one which appeared among a multitude of little pink plastic 4 mm scale pigs which have found a home elsewhere at Craig.

A busy scene at Altbeg, the small township to the south-west of Craig. A permanent-way gang is at work on the track in the foreground, while in the village street a certain amount of excitement has been caused by attempts to recapture a goat which has got over the wall on to the embankment and is munching away at the gorse bushes just to the right of the station name board. A train of East Coast six-wheelers hauled by a N.E.R. class M1 4-4-0 has just pulled into the station and passengers are making their way up the footbridge to the station offices which span the railway tracks, and look something like some of the stations on the now defunct Edinburgh suburban railway.

Altbeg nestles among the foothills of the Craigshire Highlands, but has a number of old seventeenth-century timber-framed houses (Ballard model buildings) which give the place the look, almost, of an English rather than a Scottish village. This is a little unusual, since most towns or villages near the Border do have a subtle difference in character depending upon which side of the Border they lie. Duns and Kelso, for example, seem undoubtedly Scottish, and Norham and Wooler are distinctively English.

I think the biggest mistake I made with the second layout was to get the walls of the room papered with a light blue ceiling paper. The idea, of course, was to provide a sky-blue background to Craigshire, and maybe it would have been quite a good idea if I could also have had powerful strip lighting running around the room above the layout. As it was, with just the one normal light bulb in the room, the only result was to throw a blue "cast" over everything and to destroy the original carefully worked out colour balance. It was because of this, incidentally, that I changed the livery of the C.M.R. locomotives from a dark to a fairly light green. However, the walls will not be blue much longer, for the wheel has turned full circle and once again Craigshire awaits dismantling and resurrection. I regard this event with mixed feelings because, truth to tell, the past few years have not been quite as kind to me as I should have liked, and personal worries and spells of ill-health have meant that there have been long periods

The N.B. 4-4-2 "Yorkie" pauses just outside the shale mine at Altbeg.

The fact that Altbeg shale mine looks more like a coal mine is simply explained by the fact that the buildings really were originally intended as part of a coal mine and were pressed "temporarily" into service. However, as is the usual way with so many temporary things, they are still with us, except that the pit shaft winding gear has been removed—not merely because it seemed inappropriate, but because I have a shrewd suspicion that one would never find a pit shaft quite so close to a main railway line.

during which I have had neither the time nor the inclination to do much in the way of railway modelling. I am hoping that the start of a new Craigshire will mean a new start in many ways. The mere appearance of this book is a hopeful sign, and it may even be that by the time anyone comes to read this the third Craigshire will already be arising phoenix-like from the ashes of the old.

Needless to say, the plans for it have been fermenting for quite a long time, and I am, of course, quietly confident that the third Craigshire will be much better than its predecessors! Every railway modeller worth his salt is sure that his *next* layout is going to see the fulfilment of all his dreams and ambitions. He may know at the back of his mind that once he has actually built the layout he will discover a whole host of better ways he could have done things—but this

merely provides the excuse for trying again at a later date. Indeed, as Alice discovered, it is always jam tomorrow but never jam today. And this is as it should be. The true modeller is never completely satisfied, and is always looking for new worlds to conquer. As in my own case, circumstances may actually force him to give up modelling altogether for several years, but once an interest in railways has been found, and once that interest has found expression in railway modelling, there is no going back. The modeller may have to dispose of his layout and devote himself to family or other commitments, but the germ will always be there lying dormant. One day he will pick up a copy of the "Railway Modeller" from his local newsagent or bookstall, the next day perhaps he will buy himself a wagon kit "just for the fun of it", and almost before he knows what is happening the first bits and pieces for a new layout will be being assembled. There is no escape. I myself am now reconciled to the fact that the Craig and Mertonford Light Railway will always be with me in one way or another and, who knows, maybe one day the ultimate Craigshire really will blossom forth in some Elysian field. And until that day comes? Well, one can always keep on trying. . . .

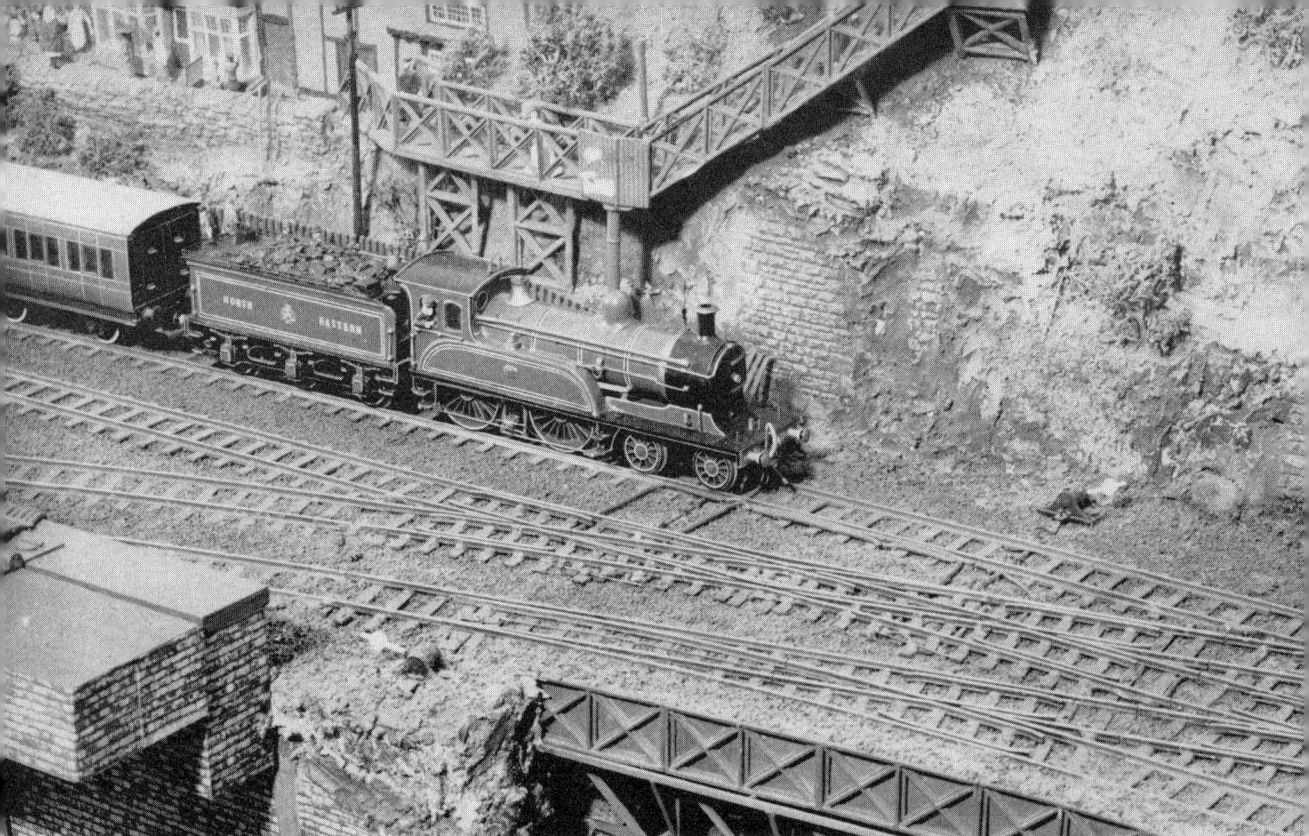

8   I like locomotives

Another view of the N.E.R. 4-4-0 at Altbeg. Station Road stretches only a little way along the side of the Up station platform and then comes to a dead end. The only ways out are either along the railway track (forbidden!) or else (for pedestrians only) by means of the footbridge which the railway company has erected to by-pass the old right-of-way which used to cross the river lower down.

Even in this day and age of the ubiquitous motor car the railways still exercise their fascination over a wide diversity of people. Not so very long ago, when I was travelling back to Mallaig on the West Highland line after a day spent near Lochailort, a small boy had literally to be dragged from the train at Arisaig, while his parents tried frantically to staunch his tears with promises that they would come back to travel on the train another day. For people of my generation much of the romance of our railways has gone with the passing of the steam locomotive, yet here was this small boy, who had never seen a steam locomotive in his life, still moved profoundly by the sight and sound of, and by the actual experience of travelling in a train—even though the train was hauled merely by one of those yellow-fronted, diesel-powered boxes on wheels!

He was quite right, of course; and it is I who am wrong to imagine that a railway without the steam locomotive has lost its power to rouse the emotions. Indeed, I know that this is not so, because every rail journey which I make is still something to be savoured and enjoyed, and something precious has been lost if a day's outing to the countryside has had to be made by car or bus instead of by the customary train. And there have been occasions—especially on the Highland and the West Highland lines—when I have even felt a very faint twinge of something almost like affection for the rather dirty Sulzer diesel hauling me along!

Nevertheless, for all those who knew it, it is the steam locomotive which remains for ever enshrined at the heart of the railway system, and it was obviously a desire to recapture something of the glory of the great days of steam which helped me to take the decision to turn Craigshire into a pre-Grouping layout. It would have been more natural in many ways—and easier—to have modelled the era I actually knew. But for most of my life the railway story has been a sad one, and the locomotives during the last days of steam have also been sad and uncared for. There would have been something a little painful

63

"Angus" and the late evening train to Dundreich and all stations to Mertonford. On the hillside near Dundreich.

in portraying them thus, and so I have looked back to the Golden Age which I never knew, but which I am pleased to say I did manage to glimpse from time to time.

I remember, for example, sitting on a platform seat at Aberystwyth one fine June day in 1959 and feasting my eyes upon "Dunley Manor" waiting to depart with the "Cambrian Coast Express." This was the very first really spotless locomotive I had ever seen in actual regular service. It was spotless not because it had just emerged from the paint shops, but because it had been well looked after and kept cleaned and polished for a long time. It shone with that peculiar velvety and oily gleam which I had previously only read about in books, and which had been the hallmark of all the important express locomotives in the old pre-Grouping days. Nor was that all. The driver and fireman were also sitting on one of the platform seats just opposite the engine, having a spot of lunch in traditional manner, and every so often one of them would pick up the bit of oily rag that lay between them, and would walk over to the locomotive and give a vigorous polish to some offending part which failed to meet the high standard of cleanliness expected of it. This scene remains one of my most precious memories, and I wish I had dared to summon up the courage to get into conversation with that driver and fireman. The experience was almost enough to convert me into a G.W.R. enthusiast on the spot!

However, 1959 was also the year in which the Scottish Region of British Railways restored four of our old engines to their Pre-Grouping liveries, and even if these did not quite equal "Dunley Manor" in sartorial elegance they at least helped to keep me faithful to my modelling of the northern scene.

Yes, I do like locomotives, but it nevertheless does come as something of a shock to discover that the number of model locomotives which have now run— or in some cases not run—upon our Craigshire metals must now be round about the forty mark—which is obviously far more than is warranted by the size of the layout. I say "round about", because I am afraid that I have managed to lose track of quite a few of them over the years. A few have been "sold out of service." One very early o-6-oT*, consisting of a Stewart-Reidpath G.W.R.-type cast body and a home-made chassis cut and drilled out of a solid bar of brass (don't ask me why!) ended up upon Ken Northwood's "North Devonshire Railway" and, as far as I know, is still there. A great many more early attempts at locomotive building have simply vanished by a natural process of decay and dissolution—that is to say, part of the chassis of one model may have been found useful in the construction of another, and the bits and pieces left over have gradually dispersed themselves over the whole locomotive stock. Thus the chassis of "Dunedin II", which was the first narrow-gauge loco ever to run on the C.M.R., is still giving yeoman service in an adapted form in "Ian." The abandoned body, renamed "Douglas", spent many years as part of the monumental scrap heap which

* A photograph of it appeared on the cover of the March 1956 issue of the "Railway Modeller."

*Another view of the
Craigshire tunnel, photo-
graphed at the interesting
moment when "Angus" at the head of
two C.M.R. coaches is beginning to labour
up the embankment towards Dundreich at
precisely the same time as "Hazeldean" emerges from
the tunnel. In another moment the standard- and the narrow-
gauge trains will be running side by side, though not for very
long. . . . If "Angus" can make ten m.p.h. up the gradient
she will be doing very well indeed, whereas "Hazeldean" will
be past in a flash, doing a good sixty or seventy m.p.h.*

evolved at the back of the original locomotive shed, and even had a final hour of glory in the shape of an article entitled, "The end of the road", which appeared in the March 1953 issue of the "Railway Modeller." With the rebuilding of the layout in the early sixties the Company simply lost track of it. I have a suspicion that the chimney may have ended up on "Roderick" but where the rest is goodness only knows.

"Dunedin II" was the last of a string of three "Dunedins" which represent my very first attempts at model locomotive construction. The first was a standard-gauge 0-4-0 saddle-tank with a cardboard body which I had the temerity to describe in an article in the "Model Railway News." Looking back upon it now I realise that it did have its points of interest. The chassis, for example, was built out of

Juneero strip upon adapted Meccano principles, utilizing "double angle brackets" to hold together the side frames. The body gave early evidence of my perennial inability to do things the proper way, and instead to evolve peculiar and distinctive methods of my own. The motor was the same original-type Romford which was later transferred to "Dunedin II" and ended up in "Ian." It has since had a new armature, new brushes, and a new one of those brass strips which hold the whole thing together, but I suppose one could say it is still the same motor—at least the magnet is the original! The reason why this particular motor moved around so much in the early days was simply due to the fact that for quite a surprising time it was the only one I had, the things being virtually unobtainable for several years after the War.

Incidentally, I still find Romford motors among the most reliable—although pride of place must perhaps

The first pre-Grouping wagons at Craig were simply standard commercial vehicles re-lettered. Here an N.B.R. "C" class 0-6-0 goods loco. hauls a string of N.B. coal wagons and vans on to the main line. These are all Tri-ang vehicles, but there is also a Peco Wonderful wagon which has become a Bruce Lindsay Bros. Ltd. private owner's wagon. The hoarding in the background contains five little photographic prints of Edwardian posters.

be given to the American Pittman series. I also retain a fondness for the now obsolete Stewart-Reidpath spur-gear mechanisms which, though noisy, will grind their way through any amount of dirt on the track and keep going under conditions where other makes have given up the ghost long ago. I have had no luck at all with some of the cheaper and more generally used motors. I am not sure whether the fault is really in the motors or in me, but the fact remains that I have been unable to achieve any sort of reasonable performance with them. The reason I suspect that there must be something in me personally which puts a hoodoo on things is that I have seen these motors performing perfectly in *other* people's models.

I am afraid that my methods of locomotive construction are mostly of the kitchen table rather than the precision workshop variety, but they do produce models which work and which look reasonably like the real thing, and I have long since reconciled myself to the fact that I am never likely to produce anything to Beeson or F. J. Roche standards.

My usual material for loco side-frames is $\frac{3}{8}''$ by $\frac{1}{16}''$ brass strip. I have a suspicion that steel would be better in many respects, but I have always avoided it for fear of its beginning to rust. I usually cut the strips to the length desired, solder them temporarily together, and drill the necessary axle holes through

both at once. This is done with an ordinary hand drill, and I must confess that two or three attempts are often necessary before I get a pair of side frames with axle holes drilled properly at right angles. Only after I am satisfied that I really have, do I finish cutting them to shape. In the case of my earlier models I usually arranged for the frames to be screwed to several spacing blocks so that everything could be dismantled if necessary. However, it so rarely seemed to be necessary that now, once I have got everything right, I just solder the frames to the spacers and assume that everything will stay all right. Why shouldn't it, after all? The worst that is likely to happen is that the wheels will become sloppy in their axle holes after a few years running, and then they will have to be removed and the holes bushed— but there will probably be no need to dismantle the chassis as such.

In theory, I like the idea of the locomotive wheels being insulated on both sides so that the body itself is at neutral polarity. In practice, however, I have nearly always taken the easy way out and fitted insulated wheels and current pick-ups on one side only, leaving the other side and the body to take care of themselves. However, I never use wheels with die-cast or alloy tyres because these are so bad at picking up the current, and, if necessary, I break the insulation on Romford metal-rimmed wheels just so that I can have metal rims on the uninsulated wheels as well as on the insulated wheels. On some models I have experimented with various ways of springing the driving wheels, but in 4 mm scale I am not at all sure if this is really such an aid to good running as is sometimes made out.

Over the construction of metal locomotive bodies

I shed sweat, blood and tears, but somehow they go together in the end. Nowadays, of course, one can purchase white metal or plastic kits for practically every type and class of locomotive except the ones I want. These kits are not without their snags, but they can be assembled by the average modeller in a fraction of the time it would take to build a comparable model from scratch. It is also possible to use the kit for one locomotive as the basis for the construction of another, or two kits can be amalgamated and embellished with spare parts left over from yet a third. This is an aspect of model-making which has a curious fascination all its own. R. W. G. Bryant once coined the term "model-bashing" to describe it, and the curious thing is that the same modeller can alternate between periods of dead-scale, accurate, "serious" model making and fits of the most irresponsible "model-bashing" imaginable. Perhaps the one acts as a safety-valve to the other. Thus I have seen myself, in the middle of the construction of some model over which I am taking particular care, suddenly drop everything and spend two or three nights throwing together something like the little work-car illustrated here.

This is one of a number of oddities which have appeared on the C.M.R. from time to time, and, like so many of them, its basis was a commercial motor bogie with the wheels pushed in on the axles to suit my 9 mm narrow-gauge. The driving cab was part of a Dinky Toy mechanical horse, the mudguards and seats were simply little bits of brass sheet cut to size with scissors and bent to shape with pliers. The rest was just light-hearted embellishment. I added cab rails where they seemed necessary, built up little toolboxes out of stripwood, and hung coils of wire and lengths of chain from various bent wire hooks. Finishing touches were added in the shape of a bicycle strapped to the rear of the vehicle, and Andrew MacAlistair having forty winks on one of the side seats.

This, of course, is "model-bashing" just for fun— but the same techniques can be used quite seriously in adapting a commercial kit to one's own particular needs, and my own conversion of a Triang Southern Railway L1 body into a North British Railway "Glen" took quite a long time and was carried through with as much painstaking care as I would have given to a completely scratch-built model.

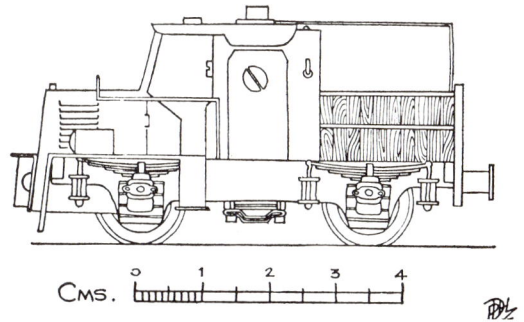

CMS. 0 1 2 3 4

4MM. SCALE PETROL - DRIVEN WORK - CAR

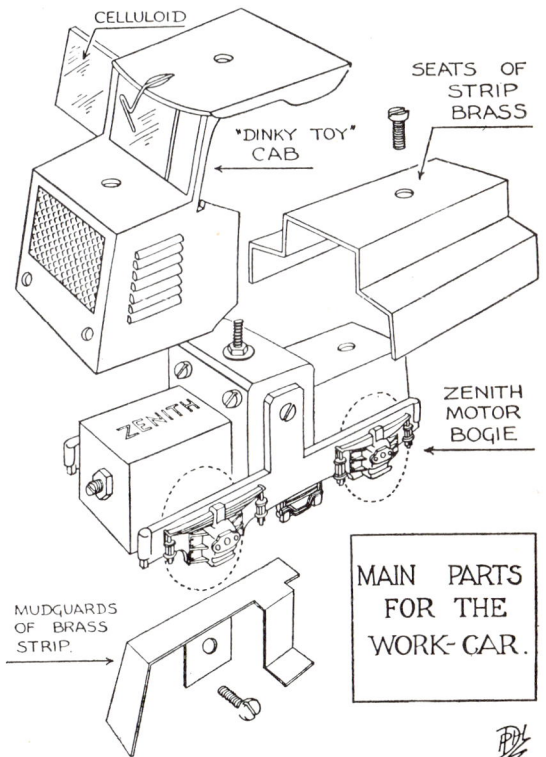

CELLULOID

"DINKY TOY" CAB

SEATS OF STRIP BRASS

ZENITH MOTOR BOGIE

ZENITH

MUDGUARDS OF BRASS STRIP.

MAIN PARTS FOR THE WORK-CAR.

Four views of the C.M.R.'s first locomotive—"Dunedin II"—later rechristened "Douglas". The design was loosely based upon that of "Blanche" on the Penrhyn Railway, and the first photograph shows the locomotive in her prime. The large saddle tank gave plenty of room for the motor, and the second photograph shows how this was mounted on its side. However the motor was eventually required elsewhere, and photographs three and four show how "Douglas" came to end her days on the scrap heap behind Craig locomotive works. The character who is looking at her, hands on hips, is driver Angus McPhwat, come to pay his last respects to his one-time charge before she is finally broken up for scrap.

9 The narrow-gauge locomotives

The construction of 4 mm scale narrow-gauge locomotives has been considerably simplified since the arrival on the scene of Arnold Rapido, Minitrix and other extremely reliable "N" gauge motors and mechanisms. None of these was available when the Craig and Mertonford was being built, and the perennial difficulty was always that of squeezing a motor into the small bodies. The usual way around this difficulty was to lay a Romford motor on its side, mount the worm-wheel on a jack-shaft, and drive on to the axle via a pair of "idler" gears. This involved redesigning the brush gear and making other minor modifications to the motor and, even so, the only way to get it into the locomotive was quite openly to build "Ian" and her immediate successors on the C.M.R. to a scale of 4.5 mm instead of 4 mm to the foot. Only in the last few years has adapted "N" gauge equipment enabled me to shrink the dimensions of C.M.R. stock to something approaching scale accuracy. Nowadays, indeed, the problem quite often operates in reverse, since Eggerbahn, Playcraft and other commercial small scale narrow-gauge models are all built to the scale of 3.5 mm to the foot, which is actually smaller than I want. Still, I must not complain, since it really is most thoughtful of the manufacturers to tailor their products to the actual track gauge which I chose so fortuitously so many years ago.

Apart from "Dunedin II"—which, anyway, was later re-christened "Douglas"—all the locomotives on the C.M.R. have been named after the various members of Lord Craig's family which, being pretty extensive, provided a ready-made reservoir of names into which the Company could dip whenever a new locomotive was ready to enter service. The little nameplates affixed to the locomotives have been photo-engraved by several of the firms which periodically advertise this work in the model railway press, and they certainly add an attractive finishing touch. One minor trouble which has emerged from the naming of the locomotives has been the problem of how to refer to them in articles. Most of the names are masculine, and yet I find that I am psychologically

"Ian"—the C.M.R.'s second "main-line" locomotive—is really an adaptation of "Douglas's" old chassis with a new body converted from a toy casting once supplied by Richard Kohnstam Ltd.

unable to refer to a locomotive as "he" or "him", and it seems equally unsuitable in most contexts to refer to "it". Locomotives, like ships, seem inexorably to be feminine! When launching a ship, the Lady Mayoress whangs the bottle against the bows and says something like, "I name this ship "Malcolm Canmore". May God bless her and all who sail in her." Her—you notice—even although the name is "Malcolm." So it is with locomotives; and hence my apparent inconsistency when I talk about "Ian" and her successors.

The C.M.R. locos are also all numbered but the numbers bear no relation to the order in which the models were actually built or acquired. They are related instead to the hypothetical order in which the Company might have received them, and numbers have been transferred as locomotives have been added or withdrawn. "Ian" has always been No. 2 and "Alistair" No. 5, but to unravel the complexities of all the number changes becomes more and more difficult with the passing years. I now fully appreciate the difficulties which railway historians have when investigating the development of some of the Colonel Stephens railways, or of other light railways where inadequate records have been kept. If I, who am responsible, cannot unravel the history of my own model railway who can? One thing I can be pretty definite about, however, is the livery of the C.M.R. locomotives. This has always been green—unlined for the first few years—but later lined out in red and yellow when I had summoned up sufficient courage to tackle the job. My lining is done with the aid of a

"Ian's" chassis—constructed along similar lines to "Alistair's"—with a rebuilt Romford motor lying on its side.

draughtsman's mapping pen and thinned down Humbrol oil colours. It is very far from perfect, but at least the later attempts are better than the earlier, so there is always hope of improvement. Recently lining transfers have become available, but in some instances I find these almost as difficult to apply as trying to draw a straight line with the mapping pen.

The green of the C.M.R. loco stud has become lighter and yellower with the passing of the years. Originally it was a very dark green—almost G.W.R. green—and this remained the official livery just so long as the particular tin of paint which I was using lasted out. This was a tin of the most remarkable paint I have ever used. I bought it in a model aeroplane shop just after the War and was never able to get any more. It was an acetone-based paint and normally I do not like these paints, but this particular blend flowed on so smoothly and evenly that one just could not go wrong with it. What was more, it never hardened or formed a skin in the tin, and seemed to be of just the same consistency at the end of its life as at the beginning—a "miracle" paint, in fact—and I often wonder who the manufacturers were and why their amazing product vanished from the market.

69

View of "Alistair's" chassis, as supplied by Cherry's Ltd., showing the specially adapted Romford motor which was built for the locomotive.

When the tin was finished I tried to match the original colour using Humbrol paints, but was not altogether successful. I then decided I would like a somewhat lighter green anyway, and most of the C.M.R. locos are now painted in the lighter shade or intermediate versions. Only "Alistair" retains the original livery, largely because I managed her lining so successfully that I am loath to strip it off.

How many narrow-gauge locos have there been on the C.M.R.? As I say, it is more than probable that I have actually lost track of some of them, but there must have been a good round dozen at the very least, and a closer look at some of them may not be out of place.

Ian. "Ian" is a 0-4-0 side tank locomotive of fairly massive proportions for a narrow-gauge loco. The body is actually a 3.5 mm scale casting of a G.W.R. "1101"-class dock shunter which was produced for the toy market in the late 'forties by Richard Kohnstam Ltd. This was a remarkably good little casting for the time, whose virtues largely went unseen and unsung. Its great virtue from my narrow-gauge point of view was the large, roomy body capable of taking a Romford motor lying on its side. The chassis is home-built from brass strip and the wheels were originally 12 mm wagon wheels mounted on PECO insulaxles, the ends of which were threaded to take screw-on outside cranks cut from $\frac{1}{32}$in thick brass sheet. After some years, however, the insulation on

the axles broke down and Nucro wheels with their little plastic insulating bushes were fitted instead. Since these used steel instead of aluminium axles there was no longer any need for the outside cranks to be screwed on the ends and they are now soldered firmly in place, thus obviating a tendency to slip out of position which had been getting worse over the years.

Alistair. "Alistair" is a model of one of the Manning Wardle 2-6-2 tank locomotives which ran on the Devonshire Lynton and Barnstaple Railway until it was closed in 1935. I never saw this railway, but I have had a fondness for the locomotives ever since I became interested in railways. There were some lovely illustrations of them in L. T. Catchpole's book* about the line, and John Ahern produced a model of "Exe" for his Madder Valley, so that it was a foregone conclusion that I should want one for the Craig and Mertonford. Indeed it is more than likely that the desire for such a model played quite a strong part in deciding me to "go narrow-gauge" in the first place.

The Manning Wardle 2-6-2s were rather complicated looking pieces of machinery, however, and my experience with "Dunedin II" and "Ian" had convinced me that my modelling capabilities were not yet sufficiently developed to enable me to tackle such a model. I therefore scraped together every available penny and got the chassis built for me by Cherry's Ltd. of Richmond, Surrey, and the body by the late

* "The Lynton & Barnstaple Railway." By L. T. Catchpole. The Oakwood Press, South Godstone, 1936.

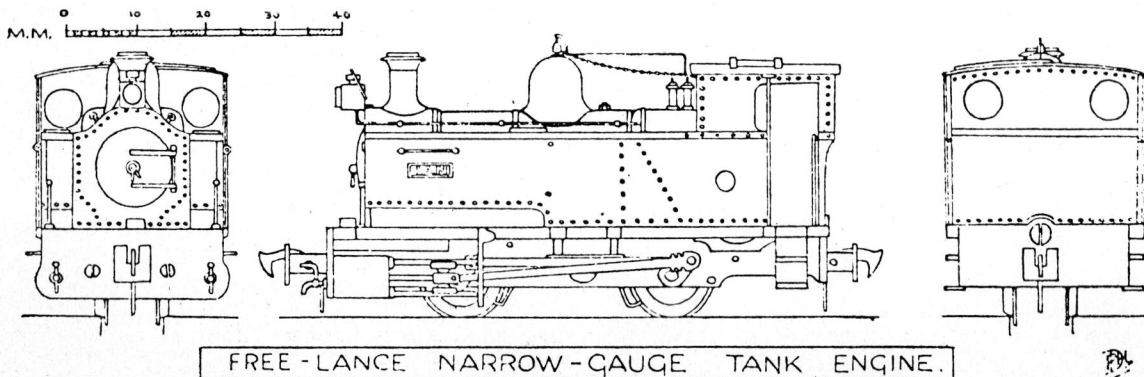

FREE - LANCE NARROW - GAUGE TANK ENGINE.

Mr. H. B. Whall (best known for his pioneering work in 2 mm scale). The final product was "Alistair" which immediately became the pride of the line and has remained so ever since. The only trouble with her as originally received was simply that she would not run! The fault was eventually traced to the specially built Romford motor and after this had been put right in the Company's workshops the loco performed faultlessly and has required very little attention since, although it must be admitted that the time has now come when she is due for a really thorough overhaul. After all, she is now over twenty years old and has probably had more actual running than any of the C.M.R.'s other locos. She is also probably the most photographed, and has the honour of having appeared on no less than four occasions on the cover of the "Railway Modeller."

One feature of "Alistair's" construction which rather surprised me when I received the chassis from Cherry's Ltd. was the fact that it had been built as an ordinary inside-framed chassis, in spite of the narrow track gauge, and the outside frames were merely dummies. This seemed a waste of space and an unnecessary complication to me, and when I later built an outside framed locomotive for myself I used the outside frames as the journals for the axles and utilized the added interior space for the current collectors.

For the major part of her life "Alistair" has been without the cowcatchers which were such a distinctive part of the originals. This was simply because they

I have always been fascinated by the Lynton and Barnstaple Railway, even although I never knew the line personally. It is perhaps not surprising, therefore, that the C.M.R. and the Lynton and Barnstaple should have much in common. Thus, just as Sir George Newnes, the newspaper proprietor, supplied much of the inspiration for the Devon line, so Lord Craig was the prime mover behind the building of the C.M.R. Both lines were opened to traffic at much the same time, and it was probably the success of the locomotive which Manning Wardle Ltd. supplied to the C.M.R. which encouraged Sir George Newnes to place an order for three identical locomotives for the Lynton and Barnstaple Railway. So successful was the design, indeed, that the Southern Railway even had another built for the Devon line in 1925. Now, alas, "Yeo", "Exe", "Taw", and "Lew" are all gone, and only "Alistair" on the C.M.R. remains to remind us of this pleasant little class of narrow-gauge locomotives. Several hands were involved in the construction of my model of "Alistair". The chassis was by Messrs. Cherrys Ltd., the body by Mr. H. B. Whall, and the paintwork and finishing touches were supplied in Craig Workshops.

got in the way of the several types of coupling which have been used on the C.M.R.—first the Rokal "TT" type, then a scale "Norwegian"-type coupler (which was very nice, but too difficult to make in quantity to be adopted for all the rolling stock) and finally the Triang "TT" hook and bar coupling. Now, however, the C.M.R. stock has all been converted to the standard Eggerbahn narrow-gauge coupling, and since this can be easily adapted, the cow-catchers will probably come back when that afore-mentioned overhaul takes place.

Mind you, even if and when the overhaul does take place, it may be that "Alistair's" days on the C.M.R. are numbered. This is because the Manning

Wardle 2-6-2s were large narrow-gauge locomotives by any standards, and "Alistair" gave the impression of being slightly overscale even when all the C.M.R.'s equipment was built to a standard 4.5 mm to the foot. As already mentioned, however, it has gradually been found possible to build new equipment much closer to a true 4 mm scale, and even to shrink some of the existing equipment. This has left "Alistair" more and more conspicuously the odd man out. What I would really like to do would be to build *another* Manning Wardle 2-6-2T, this time to strict 4 mm scale, and hand over "Alistair's" duties to her. However, the replacement would need to be a model worthy of the honour of premier place on the line, and such a model would, alas, take more time to build than I can see becoming available for quite some time in the foreseeable future. Hence the new Manning Wardle remains but a distant gleam on the horizon, and it may be a good few years yet before "Alistair" can be honourably retired to become merely a showcase model.

Angus. "Angus" started life as a Douglass Models "Welsh Pony" but has now been completely rebuilt as close to true 4 mm scale as possible. She is fitted with one of the original small K's motors and enjoys the distinction of having a flywheel which really does help to iron out her performance, and enables her to be driven along the track at a most realistic crawl. Over the years she has developed a slight waddle in her gait and a decided "clank" in her coupling rods. She also takes a little time to "warm up" after a period of inactivity—in short, a typical C.M.R. locomotive full of quirks and idiosyncrasies! At present she is No. 6 on the rosta, but I have a strange feeling that she has borne other numbers at an earlier stage of her career.

Colin and Calum. "Colin" is the name which has been borne by two C.M.R. locomotives. The first was a Triang "TT" gauge tank locomotive adapted to 9 mm gauge. It looked wrong, and was far too fast and uncontrollable. Its successor is the kind of little narrow-gauge locomotive I dreamed about for years but was only able to achieve with the advent of "N" gauge. The present "Colin" is a concoction of various bits and pieces from plastic locomotive kits on top of an Arnold Rapido 0-6-0 chassis from which

Another early photograph of "Alistair", giving an interesting view of the boiler fittings, and the little coal bunkers erected on top of the side tanks. The distinctive cowcatchers are virtually complete in this photograph, although one bit has had to be cut away from the centre of the lower bar to make room for the uncoupling bar of the Norwegian-style coupler which was originally intended to be standard on the C.M.R. Later adoption of the Triang coupler necessitated the complete removal of the cowcatcher, and this detracted considerably from "Alistair's" good looks. Now, however, the standard narrow-gauge Eggerbahn-type coupling is being fitted to all C.M.R. stock, and this will enable the cowcatchers to be reinstated.

Far Right: A posed shot of "Angus"—the third locomotive to enter service on the C.M.R. This is the original model as supplied by Douglass Models Ltd. Later on "Angus" was rebuilt to a smaller scale, but still remains considerably larger than the little Festiniog 0-4-0, "Welsh Pony" upon which the model is based.

"Colin" and "Moira"—two very short-lived C.M.R. locomotives. The first was a staid and sober adaptation of a Triang "TT" gauge 0-6-0 locomotive; the second an outrageous piece of "model-bashing" with a ridiculously short wheelbase. Both were experiments and not intended to be taken very seriously, neither of them went into proper service, and it was not long before they were broken up and cannibalized. And yet, looking at this photograph of them now, I do feel a sort of nostalgia as I remember them. "Moira", certainly, had a character all her own, and perhaps that is why, although the name "Colin" has been handed on to another locomotive, there has not yet been another "Moira."

the central pair of driving wheels have been removed, thus making the loco a 0-4-0. The low height of the motor has made it possible to have an open cab—which is something else I always used to hanker after. "Calum" is "Colin's" twin—well, more or less—since, although the chassis and boiler are the same, the passage of the years has given her a different type of cab, different boiler fittings, and other distinctive features. Both locos are very sweet running and remarkably powerful for their size. They obviously have a long life ahead of them.

Moira. Another little locomotive which has vanished from the scene is "Moira." Indeed, it is a strange thing that most of the C.M.R. locos to which I have given female names have turned out to be temperamental and somewhat unreliable in operation. Make of this what you will! Mind you, Moira was not a particularly good model anyway, having been thrown together very quickly at a time when I wanted a very short wheel-based loco in connection with a scheme for a little mine layout. "Moira" had 9 mm diameter wheels and a wheelbase of only $\frac{3}{4}$ in, so that she had no difficulty in getting around curves as sharp as 6 in radius. The motor, a somewhat battered K's job, was mounted vertically in the cab (which was the reason for what David Ronald christened the "cistern" on the cab roof.) To compensate for the weight behind the rear wheels, as much lead as possible was stuffed here, there and everywhere around the front of the loco, and "Moira" ended up by being quite powerful for her size. However, as already mentioned, she proved to be rather temperamental in operation, and was soon withdrawn from service.

Joan. "Joan" was another temperamental little loco which had a short life. She was the only diesel ever to run on the C.M.R. and was a straight-forward adaptation of a Lindsay/Kemtron "Stubby" HON3 locomotive. Her coupling rods developed an ever-increasing tendency to bind, and nothing the Com-

pany workshops could do seemed able to rectify matters. Anyway, a diesel on the C.M.R. just didn't seem right. A slightly apocryphal article in the October 1955 "Railway Modeller" described "Joan's" final break-down and ignominious withdrawal from service. The motor was pressed into service elsewhere, but what happened to the body (which was really rather a nice casting) is a complete mystery.

Duncan. "Duncan" was another C.M.R. monstrosity, but I was rather fond of her. She was a free-lance 0-4-0 vertical boilered locomotive, and was a really classic example of how *not* to build a model loco-

Another view of "Joan" outside the locomotive shed. To be perfectly fair, she was quite a pleasing looking job—as diesels go, that is!

The C.M.R. has always been pretty faithful to steam for its motive power. There have been a couple of petrol-driven railcars (one of which is still with us), but only one diesel locomotive. This was "Joan", here seen in company with "Ian" outside the locomotive shed. "Joan" was an American Lindsay/Kemtron "Stubby" 0-4-0 which was adapted to run on 9 mm gauge in Craig Workshops. Unfortunately the conversion was not altogether successful and "Joan" never ran particularly well. In the end the motor short-circuited and the mechanism jammed up solid—an event which inspired a blatant piece of anti-diesel propaganda in the "Railway Modeller" in the shape of an article entitled, "The tale of a diesel."

"Joan's" arrival at Craig attracted the interest of most of the C.M.R.'s personnel, and here Lord Craig gives them an impromptu speech, from five closely-typed pages of foolscap, extolling the virtues of dieselization. Alas for early hopes, "Joan" failed lamentably to live up to expectations, and nowadays it is hardly safe to whisper the word "diesel" in Lord Craig's presence.

Three early photographs of "Duncan"—the C.M.R.'s vertical-boilered oddity. In the first photograph "Duncan" is sporting the corrugated iron canopy which is ostensibly there to protect the driver from the rain, but which is really there to hide the enormous gear wheel which revolves just underneath it. In the other photographs both canopy and gear wheel have been removed, thus giving a much better view of the cab controls, even if rendering the locomotive inoperative. "Duncan" was never able to operate for any great length of time without resting because the resistance at the front (which enabled the 6 volt motor to be run off the normal 12 volt track supply) used to heat up very rapidly. When it became too hot to touch the operating staff knew that it was time to shunt "Duncan" into a siding and allow the paintwork to cool down and stop bubbling.

Lord Craig with "Duncan" and one of the early "Rokal" wagons.

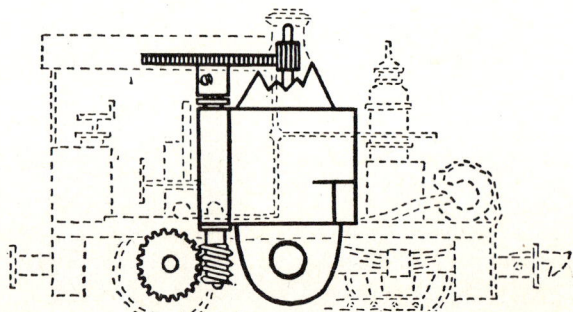

motive. Like "Moira", she was thrown together one week-end in a fit of devilment and care-free exuberance. Her chassis was held together by great blobs of solder, her wheels were uncoupled so that she slipped on the slightest provocation, and when under way she lurched and wheezed along the track in a most alarming manner.

And yet I flatter myself that all these faults did help to give "Duncan" a certain character. Her rolling gait made it appear as though her springs were weak and worn, the wheezing of her gears gave the impression that she was leaking steam at every joint, and the various "clanking" noises she made resembled those of coupling rods which had worn loose through years of hard use. In short, "Duncan" did her best to look like one of those locomotives which, odd enough at the start, had gone so often through the Company's workshops and received so many additions and alterations, that she now formed a class unique in herself. The effect was obtained largely by the accident of hurried construction, but also partly through design. In some instances I even exaggerated my bad workmanship. Thus where solder had leaked out over the cylinders and behind the buffer beams I did not clean it all away, but left little trickles and patches and worked it up to resemble caked layers of oil and dirt. Similarly when I soldered the coal bunker in place I accidentally got it on a slant, but I did not correct this since it seemed quite in character. In fact, I gave the metal sheeting one or two deliberate scale-sized dents and bashes to increase the effect!

Other touches included a drooping chain around the cab, and a cab roof consisting of a sheet of corrugated iron. The Company's books record that the chain was added in 1899, after an incident when Driver Angus MacWhirter was thrown off the foot-

plate as a result of the loco's erratic motion. The corrugated awning was not supplied until 1911—in spite of repeated entreaties by the same Angus MacWhirter who disliked being soaked to the skin every time it rained. These, at any rate, are the "official" versions—the sober facts were less romantic. The chain was there simply because it looked nice and I just happened to have some jewellery chain small enough for the job; the awning *had* to be there, because it hid an enormous gear wheel.

The reason why the gear wheel had to be where it was is shown by the drawing, which reveals that "Duncan" was powered by a cheap circular-magnet type of toy electric motor. The particular motor used was a "Mighty Midget" and this incorporated one small and one large gearwheel giving a speed reduction of 6:1. Since the worm and worm wheel gave a reduction of 25:1, this totalled up to 150:1 which meant that the loco was pretty slow. But, as I have said already, I like slow-running locomotives, and "Duncan" looked very much in place pottering about the goods yard with a couple of wagons. The motor, incidentally, was a 6 volt job and the thing that looked like a gas cylinder at the front of the loco was actually a resistance wired in series with the motor to enable it to be run off the normal 12 volt track supply.

"Agnes" and train on the timber bridge between Ormistone and Glenmuir. "Agnes" was a very American-looking locomotive with the distinction of a working headlight and a glowing firebox. She therefore spent quite a considerable part of her time ambling around the layout in the darkness, casting lurid flickering shadows on the trees and hills as she passed.

"Duncan's" wheels were 12 mm diameter disc wheels mounted on Peco insulaxles, and current was collected from them via a couple of phosphor-bronze springs. The loco side frames were two brass coach bogie castings and since these were soldered permanently to the buffer beams and footplate the only way the wheels could be removed was by cutting the axles in half and letting them drop out. This had to be done when the insulation on the insulaxles gave way and when the worm and worm wheels were required for transfer to the C. & D.E.T. Co. tramcar no. 2.

So "Duncan" is now out of commission. It would be possible to restore her to service, but this does not seem advisable in today's circumstances. "Duncan" was a good deal larger than any narrow-gauge locomotive of her type ought to have been, but this was unavoidable since there were no motors available in the early nineteen fifties which would have been small enough to let me build a scale job. As it was, the motor was mounted in an upright position to represent the

"Agnes" with the C.M.R. works wagon—another American-style vehicle, half brake-van and half open wagon, stuffed full of tools and emergency equipment.

boiler and the rest of the locomotive was built up around it so as to look reasonably correct. She was as small as it was possible to make her then. Now, however, it would be possible to use an Arnold Rapido or some other "N" gauge motor and build a new "Duncan" which would be strictly to scale and a much more worthy example of the model-maker's craft. If and when she is built I only hope, however, that she will have as much character as the original!

Agnes. "Agnes" was a 2-4-0 of obvious transatlantic origin. She entered C.M.R. service in 1955, was withdrawn a couple of years later, and suffered the usual fate of withdrawn C.M.R. locomotives by being cannibalized for spare parts. The C.M.R.'s books credited her optimistically to the Baldwin Locomotive Works, although whether they would really have been prepared to admit responsibility for her is rather doubtful. The theory, anyway, was that she was one of those American locomotives, left behind in France after the first World War, which somehow found their way across to Britain, and, being sold off at a bargain price, was immediately snapped up by Lord Craig who had her transported by sea from the south of England and up the East Coast to Craig.

The real reason for the American appearance of "Agnes" was that she was designed in order to use up as many as possible of the odd locomotive fittings which I acquired from time to time through the generosity of Leven Kemalyan of the Kemtron Products Co. of Fresno, California. In the early 'fifties this firm was a most useful source of small diameter wheels and other narrow-gauge parts for

the C.M.R. The parts were not easily obtained due to the currency restrictions then prevailing, but I managed to obtain a small dollar account in the U.S.A. as a result of writing one or two articles for the American "Railroad Model Craftsman" magazine.

One of "Agnes's" features was a large oil head-lamp housing a twelve volt pea-bulb. This made her the first locomotive on the C.M.R. to acquire the distinction of a working headlight. What is more, she had another light in the firebox shining through a piece of red celluloid. Both lights could be switched in or out of circuit by means of a small switch at the front of the locomotive, and the wiring required for this was disguised as steam pipes wandering along the side of the saddle tank and boiler in typically American fashion. The chassis of the locomotive was adapted from a Lindsay "Stubby" diesel locomotive, and the motor was a Lindsay L.580—a magnificent little piece of workmanship with a totally enclosed seven-pole armature.

Roderick. "Roderick" is a really massive 0-6-0T—another of the C.M.R.'s 4.5 mm to the foot locomotives, and the last to be completed before "N" gauge equipment revolutionized the narrow-gauge scene. Like "Alistair", "Roderick" now looks very over-size and out of place amongst the new C.M.R. equipment, and is held mainly in reserve. This is something of a pity because the loco is an excellent performer, is very smooth and slow-running (thanks to a 5-pole Japanese motor), and is capable of hauling just about anything I care to put behind her.

10 The standard-gauge locomotives

As already related, the first model locomotive I ever built was a standard-gauge 0-4-0, but once I had begun to develop the narrow-gauge C.M.R. the only standard-gauge locomotives that appeared at Craig were proprietary models, often of American or Continental origin. It was not until I decided to put back the clock to pre-Grouping days, and to make Craigshire into a combined standard and narrow-gauge layout, that I dared to tackle the construction of any "real" model locomotives—models, that is, of actual prototypes.

The narrow-gauge locomotives which I had built were all free-lance models or else merely based upon actual prototypes. To be perfectly honest, I was rather afraid of making the attempt to produce a recognizable model of a real locomotive. There was a series of articles on model locomotive construction which appeared in one of the model railway magazines at the time when I was first becoming involved in the hobby, and I think this gave me a very marked inferiority complex. The articles were aimed more at the experienced modeller than at the beginner, and to a beginner they were rather awe-inspiring. In a laudable attempt to improve the standard of modelling they frowned upon all the easy makeshifts for producing a model locomotive quickly, and I was given the impression that it would be sacrilege of the very worst sort if I were to build a chassis with plain unshaped sideframes or if I were to use bullhead rail and washers to represent coupling rods. These are, admittedly, *not* good practices, but for the beginner the adoption of such methods may make all the difference between being able to complete a model in a semi-reasonable length of time and never being able to complete it all.

N.B.R. "Kettledrummle." Even with the adoption of several of these expedients it took me all of five month's spare time to complete my first serious standard-gauge model of a North British Railway 4-4-0 "Scott" class locomotive. At the end of that time I was able to refute absolutely the contention which is sometimes made that it is just as easy to build a model of a real locomotive as to build a free-

Two views of the first "Dunedin"—a saddle tank 0-4-0 based upon a little Manning Wardle locomotive which was built for the International Exhibition at South Kensington in 1862, and described and illustrated in the January 1948 "Model Railway News." "Dunedin" had a chassis made from Juneero strip and a cardboard body. She was my very first attempt at building a model locomotive, and, in spite of all her obvious faults, I was inordinately proud of her when she first moved down the track under her own power.

lance model. My narrow-gauge models went together in half the time simply because I was able to use up any odd chimneys, domes, and bits and pieces that happened to be lying around. But for this model of N.B.R. No. 425 "Kettledrummle" there were no such easy ways out. Everything had to be carefully measured and cut to precise dimensions, commercial

The American influence which permeated Craigshire for several years was nowhere stronger than on the little bit of standard-gauge track which, in the original scheme of things, never got any further than Ormistone. Probably the most unashamedly American locomotive which appeared here was this Varney 4-6-0 "Casey Jones". In the end the American-style equipment was all demoted from Craigshire and restyled and relettered as part of the "Fort Stewart and Sierraville Railroad"—a rather unusual railway in that it ended up with four locos., three passenger coaches and several freight vehicles but nowhere to run.

The privately-owned locomotive operating the siding at Peter Allan's Processing Plant—a cut down Stewart-Reidpath tank locomotive body on top of an American Mantua "Booster" 0-4-0 chassis—the only locomotive on the pre-Grouping layout with Walschaerts valve-gear.

Long before Triang brought out their "O" gauge "Big Big" train sets, Craigshire was experimenting with a self-contained, electrically-driven diesel locomotive. The chassis is illustrated here and comprised (reading from left to right) a set of Meccano bevel gears, a model boat gear reduction unit, a Frog 3-volt electric motor, a Meccano reversing switch and four pencil-torch batteries. Believe it or not, the unit did work!

N.B.R. "Scott" class 4-4-0, "Kettledrummle", on the turntable at Craig, shortly after the layout had gone pre-Grouping.

parts had to be filed down to the right size and shape, and finally the finished model had to be painted in correct N.B. livery.

This in itself was no light task, especially as no two authorities seemed to be in agreement as to just what constituted N.B.R. "gamboge." It was a colour, apparently, which varied considerably from year to year and even from locomotive to locomotive. Eventually, however, I was able to obtain the loan of an N.B.R. colour panel from the late Sir Eric Hutchison, and worked to the best of my ability from that, using the then new Humbrol oil paints. In the various photographs the lining has not come out very well since what looks like a thick continuous line of one colour is actually two lines—red and yellow—but the red does not show up. The reader, looking at the photographs, may also notice a patch on the side of "Kettledrummle's" tender, just underneath the crest, which is of a slightly different shade from the rest of the body colour. There is quite a story behind this.

I originally christened the locomotive "Ivanhoe"—largely because out of all the possible names for an N.B. "Scott"* this seemed one of the easiest to paint on 4 mm scale locomotive splashers. Unfortunately, I had not realized that "Ivanhoe" had been one of the very first of the "Scott" class locomotives to be built, whereas the plans from which I had been working had been of the later super-heated class. Hence I had installed triangular windows at

* There were 43 "Scott" class 4-4-0s built by the N.B.R., all named after characters in the Waverley novels by Sir Walter Scott.

the front of the cab instead of the round windows with which "Ivanhoe" should have been fitted. This fact was gleefully pointed out to me by quite a number of folk to whom I showed the finished model.

So it was either change the cab windows or change the name, and changing the name seemed a great deal easier. I could, no doubt, have had another fairly short name (such as "Norna") had I wanted, but I thought I might as well be adventurous and see if I could possibly manage to squeeze "Kettledrummle" on to the splasher. Why "Kettledrummle"? Well,

"Kettledrummle's" super-detailed bogie, with sprung axleboxes and self-centring pivot unit. The over-thick plastic wheels came from a Kitmaster "Schools" class loco. because they were the only 14 mm diameter wheels I was able to obtain with the correct number of spokes. They have since been replaced by thinner Nucro metal wheels with plastic spoke inserts.

When Alisdair MacAndrew the "roving cameraman" of the "Craigshire Daily Advertiser and Gazette" wished to get some really effective photographs for the newspaper's series on "Our modern railways" he went to an embankment somewhere between Edinburgh and Craig and photographed the first trains that came along.

First on the scene was "Kettledrummle", temporarily demoted from passenger duties to haul the early morning goods to Dunbar. The echoes of her passing had hardly died away before there came a shrill whistle in the distance heralding the approach of a Newcastle express. A moment later an immaculate N.B. Atlantic stormed up the embankment with a train of mixed North British and North Eastern coaches and, right at the end, a solitary fish wagon all the way from Mallaig. Finally came an unusual visitor in the shape of a short Caledonian Railway breakdown train hauled by a 0-4-4 tank engine. Something, evidently, had gone wrong somewhere to cause a "Caley" train to be diverted on to N.B. lines, but, whatever it was, it was none of Alisdair's business. He packed up his tripod, camera, and slides and slid down the embankment to where Sandy Ogilvie was waiting with the horse and trap to take him to the nearest station. It had been a most successful little expedition.

simply because "Kettledrummle" was the first N.B. "Scott" with which I ever became acquainted. The meeting took place in Perth station several years before I had become particularly interested in railways, and it suddenly dawned upon me that the locomotive I was looking at was obviously of pre-Grouping vintage, and I wondered at the time just what its story was and to which company it had belonged. Well, now I know—and long may her miniature replica continue to run to and fro between Dunbar and Craig.

But all this, you say, still does not explain the patch on the tender. No, it does not, and I apologize for digressing, but I am just coming to the point now.

As "Ivanhoe", you see, the model had been painted in the N.B. style of immediate pre-Grouping days, with the loco number on the side of the tender; but when I decided to change the name I decided also to revert to the earlier N.B. livery with the crest between the letters N.B. Therefore "Ivanhoe's" number had to be scraped off, and the place where it had been repainted. However, I had considerable difficulty in mixing up a new lot of paint to match the existing body colour and the final result is the patch—not really noticeable under ordinary viewing conditions—but, once again, shown up by the photographs.

Since I was trying to make an extra-special job of "Kettledrummle", I incorporated a number of experimental ideas in the construction. For example, the brass sideframes of the chassis were insulated from each other by Tufnol spacing blocks, and the wheels were insulated by means of the split-axle method. That is to say, they were mounted on ordinary steel axles as though for three-rail working and the axles were then cut and pressed into short lengths of fibre tube which in their turn were forced into lengths of brass tubing in order to hold everything firm. This method of construction meant that there were no current pick-ups in the normal sense. The current was collected via the wheels, axles and sideframes on one side of the locomotive, and returned via the wheels, axles and sideframes on the other. Leads from the two motor brushes were soldered direct to the two sideframes.

The motor fitted was an American Pittman DC 60, and this drove the wheels via two-stage reduction

gearing. The first stage originally consisted of a Romford 40:1 worm and worm wheel, and the second of two clock gears with a ratio of about 3:1. This resulted in a final ratio of about 120:1 which would have been fine for a goods locomotive never expected to get beyond about a scale 30 mph but was a bit too slow for a passenger engine—even for me with my mania for slow-running locomotives. So the worm and worm wheel were changed for a set with a ratio of about 20:1, and things became a little more realistic, although even today "Kettle-drummle" is incapable of any fancy turns of speed, and cannot be used for double-heading duties with my N.B. Atlantic, "Hazeldean". This honour has

to be given instead to No. 149. "Glen Finnan" which is a pity, not only because "Glen Finnan" is not such a well-made model, but because a Glen and an Atlantic together are not so characteristic of N.B. practice as a Scott and an Atlantic.

N.B.R. "Hazeldean." For anyone modelling the North British Railway the ultimate possession is, of course, a model of one of the N.B. 4-4-2 Atlantic locomotives introduced by W. Reid in 1906. It may seem strange that the N.B. should have had these Atlantics built for them by the North British Loco-motive Company at a time when other railways were experimenting with Pacific type locomotives, but these locos were intended for the main line to

The N.B.R. "C" class 0-6-0 locomotive, consisting of an adapted Triang plastic body on top of a Stewart-Reidpath chassis. The tender does not look at all like a genuine North British one—it must, surely, have been taken over from the old Craigshire Northern Railway.

Aberdeen and for the Waverley Route to the Borders, and the latter line in particular abounded in sharp curves which, it was felt, could be more easily tackled by a four-coupled rather than by a six-coupled locomotive.

One of the Reid-built N.B.R. 0-6-2 tank ocomotives outside Altbeg shale mine. This is actually a cut-down version of one of the original Hornby Dublo tank locomotives, with new boiler and other fittings.

The Atlantics were massive machines. Aesthetically they were not so pleasing as the elegant Scotts, Glens, and other 4-4-0s, but their large boilers and squat chimneys gave them a sense of power and purposefulness. They looked powerful and (even if their consumption of coal was rather extravagant) they *were* powerful! It must have been a magnificent sight to have seen one of them storming up past Steele Road on the Waverley Route or rumbling across the Forth Bridge on the way north, and it is sad that nothing came of the plans to preserve one for posterity.

As already mentioned, my own Atlantic is a model of No. 787 "Hazeldean", and this was built for me

by Mr. A. S. Reidpath of Stewart-Reidpath Ltd. I cannot remember precisely what the cost was, but I know that it was remarkably reasonable, and in return for what I paid I received a solidly built locomotive, albeit with no frills, but also with no faults. It must have been among the last few models built by Mr. Reidpath, for I was saddened to read of his death only a few short months after receiving the model.

Stewart-Reidpath Ltd. was one of the pioneer firms producing "HO" and "OO" equipment in Britain. It was a small firm dealing only in basic essentials such as wagon and coach underframe castings and a range of excellent locomotive driving wheels. It also produced a couple of good, heavy tank locomotive castings, and a very reliable, though noisy, spur-gear driven mechanism. Needless to say, it was one of these which was fitted to "Hazeldean" and the fact that the motor was somewhat noisy and "growly" somehow seemed quite in character with the atmosphere surrounding an N.B. Atlantic.

N.B.R. Goods Locomotives. The first pre-Grouping goods locomotive to appear in Craigshire was more in the nature of a "model bashing" exercise than a serious model. It consisted of the body casting of a Triang 0-6-0, suitably messed about, and mounted on top of a ready-to-run Essar mechanism. The final result was meant to be a North British "C" class loco (unnumbered)—but, to be on the safe side, maybe I had better say that it was an ex-Craigshire Northern loco! It has now been scrapped—perhaps a bit prematurely—because I now feel the lack of an N.B.R. 0-6-0 tender loco, and the "S" class 0-6-0 which was intended to replace it is still a very long way from completion. I do, however, have quite a variety of tank locomotives, again all adaptations of commercial models, since until very recently there was a strange dearth of kits for actual N.B. prototypes, as opposed to the seeming superfluity of kits available for that rival concern, the Caledonian Railway!

Thus there is an "A" class 0-6-2 tank locomotive adapted from an old Hornby Dublo 0-6-2 Southern Railway tank locomotive. The boiler of this was lowered by the simple expedient of sawing out a whole section lengthways just above the footplate, and then glueing the remaining halves of the body together again with Araldite. More straightforward adaptations were the conversion of an ordinary

N.B.R. 4-4-2 "Yorkie" tank locomotive gently simmering outside Craig West signal box waiting for the right of way, The signal cabin could conceivably be of genuine North British design, although in actual fact it is an American plastic kit—and a very nice one, too.

Stewart-Reidpath 0-6-0 tank loco casting into a "D" class 0-6-0, and of a Stewart-Reidpath "Gnat" saddle-tank into a really quite presentable "G" class 0-4-0.

The N.B. kits which have now become available are all from GEM Models. In 1972 kits became available for the "D" class 0-6-0T and for the "K" "Glen" class 4-4-0, and in early 1973 there appeared a kit for the "C" class 0-6-0 tender loco. Examples of all these are slowly evolving in Craig workshops at the time of writing.

N.B.R. "Glen Finnan." Meanwhile I do actually possess a "Glen" of sorts in the shape of No. 149 "Glen Finnan." The basis for this was the body of a Triang Southern Railway "L1" 4-4-0, the proportions of which were not too dissimilar from those of a "Glen". The original cab was cut away, and a new cab, wheel splashers, and other details were fabricated from polystyrene sheet. This was a serious attempt to build a decent locomotive body out of plastic sheet, and I suppose that the final result was quite creditable. However, when I consider the time and labour I expended over the body, I think I would have done much better to have attempted a metal body, scratch-built in the more "normal" manner. I cannot help feeling that the plastic body somehow lacks the "sharpness' of its metal counterpart, and I miss the valuable built-in weight which a metal body would have had.

"Glen Finnan's" original chassis was merely the Triang chassis adapted to the correct wheel-spacing and fitted with new scale wheels. However this performed very badly, being far too fast and uncontrollable, and showing a marked tendency to stick on the slightest provocation. I tried fitting a Romford

motor in place of the original Triang motor, but things seemed no better. It was, indeed, during the course of this operation that I began to develop the suspicion that "Glen Finnan" was going to be one of those models I get from time to time which seem to have a definite hoodoo upon them. What happened was that I was drilling and tapping a couple of holes in the loco sideframes. At one stage in these proceedings I had to change over from a number 50 twist drill to a number 55 twist drill, and then back again. I took the number 50 drill out of the chuck and laid it down. I put in the number 55 and drilled my hole. I took out the number 55 drill and put out my hand for the number 50 drill. It wasn't there! Ten seconds ago I had put it down just there on my right. It couldn't have rolled away—there was nowhere for it to roll to. It couldn't have blown away—twist drills don't blow away. It had, unaccountably, just vanished into thin air! Needless to say, it was the only number 50 drill I had, and I wasted an hour hunting for the wretched thing. The only fortunate aspect of the affair was that it happened on a Saturday afternoon, and so I was able to go out and buy another drill—but the gremlins responsible for the outrage never replaced the original drill!

This, as I say, should have warned me; but I went on to build an entirely new chassis for "Glen Finnan" —a perfectly normal chassis, orthodox in every respect, except for the fact that it would not work when placed underneath the body. After fiddling about with it for several months I removed it and eventually transferred it to another locomotive body underneath which it performed faultlessly. The ultimate solution for "Glen Finnan" turned out to be one of the ever-faithful "Essar" mechanisms, although even this has never seemed altogether happy in its work!

N.B.R. 4-4-2T No. 26. The "Yorkies"★ were a type of N.B. locomotive with which I had no personal acquaintance, although I did make a special trip to Dundee in March 1959 to photograph the last of them standing forlornly by the engine sheds, awaiting

★ So nicknamed because built by the Yorkshire Engine Co. during 1911–1913.

N.E.R. class M1 4-4-0 No. 1621 on the turntable. This was my second attempt at building a proper scale model, and I tried my hardest to turn out something good. The result is probably a little better than "Kettledrummle." It certainly doesn't approach exhibition standards, but at least I can contemplate it with some pleasure when I reflect that it is not just a kit of commercial parts stuck together but is, in fact, virtually "all my own work."

scrapping. They were 4-4-2 tank engines used on suburban and branch line trains all over the N.B. system—obviously a most useful locomotive to have in model form—and I would probably have attempted to make one for myself sooner or later had I not managed to spot one advertised for sale in one of the model railway magazines. I half expected it to be sold before my letter reached the advertiser—but, no—I was lucky; and No. 26 entered service in Craigshire. She has been overhauled a bit, and repainted, and now has a Hornby Dublo motor in place of the Triang with which she was originally fitted.

N.E.R. Class M1 4-4-0 No. 1621. The partnership between the North British Railway and the North Eastern Railway was sometimes friendly and sometimes acrimonious. It was most apparent in the Border regions where the N.B.R. sent down invading feelers into England in the shape of the lines to Hexham and Rothbury, while the N.E.R. secured for itself through-running rights to Edinburgh. In Craigshire the relationship is obvious in the large numbers of N.E.R. locomotives and trains which may be seen round about Craig, and so it is fortunate that I myself happen to have an interest in and a liking for the old N.E.R.

In point of fact, I became acquainted with the railways of the north-east of England long before I knew those of Scotland, since after my mother and I were evacuated from Malta in the early days of the last War we came to live, first of all, in Darlington, which, as every railway enthusiast knows, was the home of the world's first public railway—the Stockton and Darlington. At that time it was the home also of the great locomotive works of Stephenson, Hawthorne and Co., "Locomotion No. 1" stood on the platform at Darlington Bank Top station, and from there railway lines still radiated in all directions. In those days it would have been possible to have travelled from Darlington to the Lake District via Barnard Castle and Kirkby Stephen, across Deepdale and Belah viaducts. This would have been a very fine thing to have done, but I did not know it at the time and, even if I had, would not have been able to

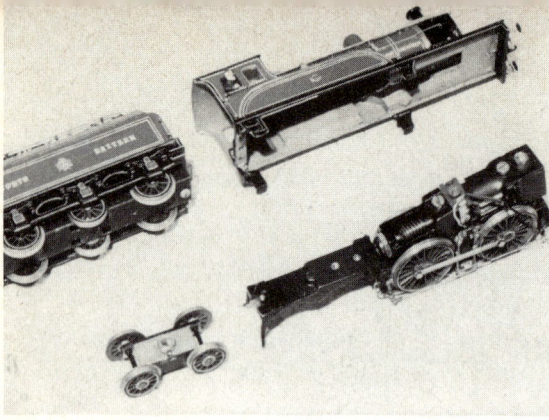

No. 1621 stripped for servicing, showing the adapted Hornby Dublo G.W.R. "castle" chassis.

afford such a jaunt. Now the opportunity is gone for ever, and I still regret it.

However, we do still have the railway museum at York, and it is possible to spend a pleasant afternoon there, gloating over the preserved glories of the North Eastern and a few other lesser railways. Of all the locomotives there my favourite is the "M1" class 4-4-0 No. 1621—one of the locomotives designed by Wilson Worsdell which so distinguished herself during the really rather reprehensible "race to the north" in 1895. However, it is not her fame which makes me so fond of No. 1621, but her beautiful proportions. Everything from the top of her well-shaped chimney to those large combined splashers over the driving wheels, seems just right. It was quite inevitable that I should want to tackle a model of her some time.

Presumably I had managed to learn something from the construction of "Kettledrummle" because 1621 took a much shorter time to build and there seemed to be no serious snags to overcome. On the other hand, maybe I was just lucky. The body was built out of brass tube and sheet along perfectly orthodox lines, but, as usual, the boiler fittings caused me a certain amount of trouble. Over the years I have managed to accumulate quite a collection of odd chimneys, domes, safety valves and other miniature locomotive parts, but when it comes to finding fittings suitable for a particular model nothing seems to be quite right, and I laboriously have to make what I want by filing a dome to a new shape or lengthening a chimney by cutting it in half, remounting the ends on a length of tubing, and making up the required thickness by wrapping sellotape around the middle. These, at any rate, were the methods adopted for 1621's dome and chimney. As for the polished brass safety valve cover, this was made from a suitable laundry collar stud painted a golden brass colour.

The beadings around the splashers, behind the smoke box, and around the cab windows were made from brass wire filed flat on one side and sweated into place with a soldering iron. I daresay there are neat and easy ways of doing both these operations, but I have not yet found them. I filed the brass wire by holding it in the vice and filing a little bit at a time as I moved it along. Sweating the final half-round strip on to the splashers resulted in quite a bit of excess solder leaking out on each side, and this had to be laboriously cleaned up with the aid of scrapers and files. This is probably an operation where practice makes perfect, and it would probably be worth it to practise for a while on spare bits of metal, just to get the knack of it, before tackling the real job. One thing I have found is that it is a mistake to use too small a soldering iron for a job like this—indeed, the bigger the better— since this enables the job to be done with one swift application of the iron, which spreads the solder nice and evenly, and avoids the danger of the iron being held in contact with the work for so long that all the previously made joints come adrift and the whole model falls apart!

1621's chassis started life under a Hornby Dublo "Castle", the body of which found a more suitable home elsewhere. The left-over chassis was suitably shortened and extra holes had to be drilled for one set of driving wheels, but otherwise very little alteration was necessary. The motor was one of the rather neat, small motors which Hornby used before they introduced the large, cab-filling "ring-field" motor, and I wish I had managed to acquire another one or two, since they operate extremely reliably and fit easily into quite confined spaces. The driving wheels utilized were Stewart Reidpath's brass wheels of the type brought out immediately after the war. These had an excellent profile and the correct number of spokes for most pre-Grouping locos. Indeed, I so much prefer them to other makes of troublesome, non-concentric, and wobbly driving wheels that some years ago I inserted an advertisement for them in the "wanted" column of the "Railway Modeller" and, as a result, managed to acquire a jealously guarded little stock-pile which should see me through the construction of three or four more models at least. (Further specimens will always be gratefully received!) One of the incidental advantages of these wheels is that the brass of which they are made seems to be an

N.E.R. class "T" 0-8-0 locomotive revolves slowly on the old gallows-type turntable at the first Craig after the long haul up from the Durham coalfields.

especially good conductor of electricity, and this helps the current pick-up immensely. In the case of 1621 the pick-up was actually arranged through the brake shoes pressing upon the treads of the driving wheels—an arrangement which I thought rather neat and ingenious—but which, alas, was not quite effective enough, so that I was forced to fit little wire pick-ups as well. A pity!

One feature which I am rather keen on in my model locomotives is some form of side-springing on leading or trailing bogies. This guides the locomotives gently into curves and prevents that excessive overhang which one so often gets at the front of a model locomotive rounding a curve, due, of course, to the fact that model bogies usually flop about quite loosely and do no work at all. In the case of 1621 there is a slot in the centre of the bogie frame so that the bogie can slide from side to side on the centre pivot, but this movement is dampened by a pair of tiny compression springs. Another spring bears down on top of the bogie, so that it does support some of the weight of the loco body. In other words, 1621 is a genuine 4-4-0 with the bogie functioning as it ought to function instead of merely coming along for the ride.

Incidentally, 1621 is painted in the "apple-green" which a number of independent experts assure me is the correct North Eastern green for the 1912 era. This is not the green in which the real 1621 presently appears at York Railway Museum, but the green seen to best advantage on the large-scale model 0-6-0 in the glass case facing the souvenir bookstall!

N.E.R. Class T 0-8-0 No. 2121. My North Eastern Railway 0-8-0 is one of the "splendid Gateshead giants" eloquently described by Mr. F. C. Hambleton in his book, "Locomotives Worth Modelling." It is, in other words, a model of No. 2121, one of the "T" class goods locomotives which were built at Gateshead in 1901 for the north-east coal traffic, and which first appeared in all the full glory of passenger style livery complete with brass capped chimneys and polished brass safety valve covers.

The basis of my model was another Hornby Dublo chassis—that for the Midland Region 2-8-0. As was the case with the chassis for No. 1621 this

had the convenient small-sized motor, and very little needed to be done beyond the fitting of scale wheels, new cylinders, slide bars, and connecting rods. However, the gearing was fiddled a bit so as to incorporate a system of two-stage reduction gearing as part of my perpetual quest for ultra slow-running goods locomotives. The current pick-up was arranged by a method very popular in the United States whereby the current is collected by the wheels on one side of the locomotive and returned by the wheels on the other side of the tender. This necessitates an insulated draw-bar between locomotive and tender, but does away with the need for any contacts rubbing against the wheels.

2121 is quite a good example of the peculiarities of my modelling methods, since the body was constructed of brass and the tender of bits and pieces left over from Kitmaster plastic kits. There was no particular reason for this except that the Kitmaster parts were too good to waste, and helped to speed construction. The difference in materials is not at all noticeable. Indeed, I had virtually forgotten all about it until I came to re-examine the model preparatory to writing these paragraphs.

Again, the boiler fittings caused quite a bit of trouble, especially the brass safety valve cover. Since this was very much larger than that used on 1621 I was unable to find a large enough collar stud for the job and ended up by filing a white metal dome down to the new shape, painting it gold, and polishing it to get as "brassy" a texture as possible. The result is not quite right, and I wish I had gone the whole hog and just filed a brass dome to shape while I was about it. I am still searching for a really successful method of achieving a good brass finish on non brass surfaces.

It is gratifying to be able to record that 2121 is

capable of hauling a fair-sized train of my heavy, very far from free-running goods vehicles—but, alas, her performance falls far short of that of the prototype. The original "T" class 0-8-0s regularly used to handle loaded trains of 1,200 to 1,300 tons, and were expected to haul sixty or so empty coal wagons up the initial 1 in 47 gradient out of Tyne Dock.

Modellers of the North Eastern Railway have been just a little bit more fortunate than modellers of the North British Railway in the number of white-metal locomotive and wagon kits which have become available over the years. One of the first N.E.R. loco kits to appear was K's kit for the "E1" class 0-6-0 tank locomotive which was for long the standard shunting loco on the North Eastern. The E1s, or J 72s as they later became, were remarkably successful engines. Seventy-five of them were built by the N.E.R., another ten were built by the L.N.E.R. in 1925 and—most remarkably—yet another twenty-eight were built by British Railways after nationalization. Two of them acted as station pilots at Newcastle station during the last years of steam, and were latterly painted in the full glory of N.E.R. green, with black and white lining, polished brasswork, and both N.E.R. and British Railways crests on the side tanks.

Needless to say, a model of one of these little 0-6-0s has found its way into Craigshire, where it may even be found doing a turn of passenger duty on one of the local stopping trains between Berwick-upon-Tweed and Craig.

Then there are George E. Mellor's kit for the "R 1" class 4-4-0, and Nu-Sto Scale Model's kit for the "T 2" class 0-8-0. Models of both of these will no doubt appear on Craigshire metals at some time in the future. But when? There are a great many jobs which have far more urgent priority than these

locomotives, and I already have more locomotives than can be used on the layout at any one time. And yet, as I say, I just happen to like locomotives, and I have no doubt that I shall go on building them for many years to come—to the scandalous neglect of all the thousand and one other things which ought to be done. This applies not merely to the North British and North Eastern locomotives, which have a legitimate place in Craigshire, but also to all the other odd interlopers which I have been unable to resist over the years. The official history of Craigshire does, it is true, make mention of a branch of The Caledonian Railway reaching Craig, and this gives me my excuse for a Caley 4-4-0 tank locomotive and for one of the Wills "Finecast" 0-6-0 Caledonian tanks. It might just be possible, moreover, to think up some sort of reason for the occasional appearance of a Bec Models Great Central Railway "Director" class 4-4-0, but what can one say about an A 3 Pacific, a K3 2-6-0, or —horror of horrors—the Anbrico twin-car diesel-unit which occasionally used to rattle around the layout when no one was looking? The trouble is that my personal railway interests do not stop short at 1912, and at times I have actually considered the possibility of Craigshire becoming two layouts in one! After all, it is surprising how little had to be altered when I first put the clock back to pre-Grouping days and, with just a little extra effort, I could quite easily have things so that a few minutes substitution here and there could effect the change from pre-Grouping to present day, and vice versa. Rolling stock would be split up into pre- and post-Grouping equipment, and one half carefully salted away while the other half was in use. Certainly the narrow-gauge side of things would present no problem at all, since the C.M.R. would continue to look just the same whether the year was 1912 or 1984!

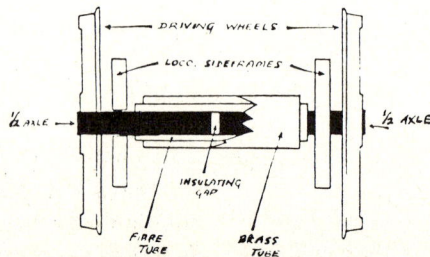

Arrangement of split axles

11 The Craigshire landscape

As the C.M.R. climbs up into the mountains an ever-increasing number of bridges are required to carry the line across small burns and rivulets. Here is a very simple wooden affair just outside Dundreich. Just above it another little planked bridge carries the footpath.

The primary purpose of a railway is to transport goods and people from one place to another. To the railway enthusiast, however, the railway is also something to be looked at and admired—either from a distance as it passes through the countryside, or else at close quarters from the station platform or from the precincts of the locomotive depot. One has the feeling, indeed, that for a good many car-owning enthusiasts of the present day this external view of the railway is their main contact with it. They will undoubtedly travel on the occasional Society-sponsored "fan" trip, but this is not quite the same thing as using the railway for normal everyday travel, and I am grateful that I can remember the railways from the pre-Beeching days when it was still possible to regard them as a national "network" and as the obvious means of getting about the country. I belong, I suppose, to the last generation whose mental picture of Britain is one of many districts linked by railway routes rather than by roadways. When people say to me that such and such a place is "on the A 66", I look at them blankly and ask, "Where's that?" and then, "Oh, you mean just south of Culgaith on the Midland Route"—whereupon it is their turn to look blank.

In the past twenty years the railway has taken me to many lovely parts of Britain which are no longer accessible by train. Quite a few of them, indeed, are no longer easily accessible by any form of public transport at all, so that my chances of seeing them again are very remote. My memories of Appin and of the Yorkshire Dales, of Liddesdale and of Ripon Cathedral, are all tied up with memories of train journeys to and from those places. For Liddesdale (and indeed for the whole Border region) I still grieve sorely, and wish more than ever that I had an enormous space at my disposal, so that I could let my scenic modelling aspirations have full play, and could let Craigshire recall for me some of the well-remembered features of the Waverley Route.

Every railway modeller, of course, hankers after a space as large as the village hall in which to build the layout of his dreams, even if he does realize that,

were he to be granted such a space, he could never live long enough to build the layout—not, that is, unless he were content to keep it very simple. After twenty-five years of railway modelling I know what I would do if I were to be given that space by some fairy Godmother. Craig and the other modelled localities would remain much as they are but the length of track between them would be stretched to the maximum. I like to dream of several scale miles of single line narrow-gauge track meandering through a model landscape of hills and woods, across bridges and through tunnels, passing a little lochan here or a lonely farm steading there. There would be one or two sidings to lineside industries and a few passing loops, but nothing else to complicate the trackwork so that, in spite of its length, there would be no maintenance difficulty. The particular enjoyment in such a large layout would come from being able to walk along beside a train as it was travelling and being able to enjoy each and every aspect of the journey as it came along.

I myself can recollect seeing two model railways on exhibition where something like this was possible. The first was the British railways layout at the Empire Exhibition in Glasgow in 1938, but since I was only

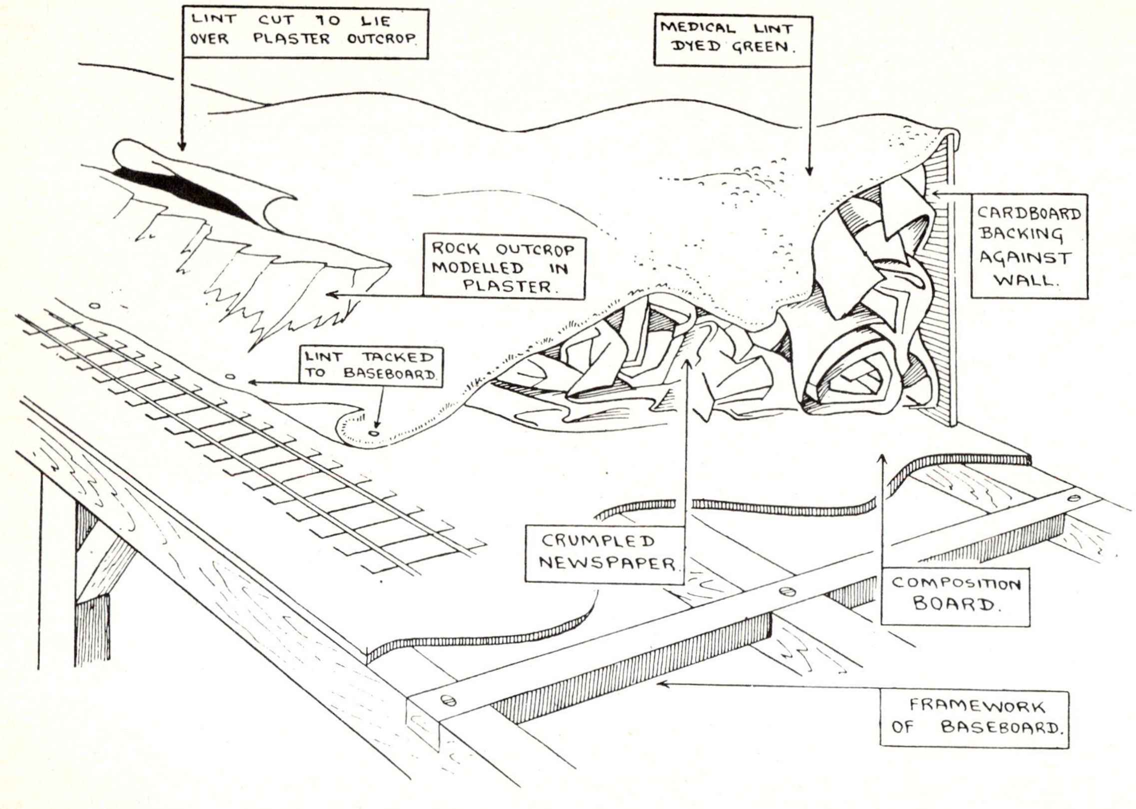
LINT CUT TO LIE OVER PLASTER OUTCROP
MEDICAL LINT DYED GREEN.
CARDBOARD BACKING AGAINST WALL.
ROCK OUTCROP MODELLED IN PLASTER.
LINT TACKED TO BASEBOARD.
CRUMPLED NEWSPAPER
COMPOSITION BOARD.
FRAMEWORK OF BASEBOARD.

Landscape modelling using dyed medical lint over rolls of crumpled newspaper.

a small boy at the time it may have seemed more impressive than it really was. If I remember rightly it consisted of a long series of dioramas linked by the trains passing through them, and it seemed to me at the time to be of truly enormous extent. The second instance was an "N" gauge layout exhibited in St. Cuthbert's Church Halls, Edinburgh, in April 1972†. This represented part of the West Highland Railway and consisted simply of a recognizable—albeit somewhat adapted—version of Mallaig, and an accurate representation of Glenfinnan Station, the two being linked by a scale mile or so of single line track passing through an autumnal Highland landscape. The whole thing was very well modelled and an excellent example of the scenic possibilities of the small gauge. If, moreover, the crowds of spectators had been less it would have been possible to have walked alongside a train on its way from Mallaig to Glenfinnan and to have enjoyed its passage by "mountain, moor and loch", as the original 1894 guide to the line had it*.

So much for dreams. Craigshire still remains confined to a space 12 ft by 10 ft, and my scenic modelling aspirations have to be kept strictly within bounds. Perhaps this is just as well, because a really effective model landscape can take a surprisingly long time to produce. The only way I know of getting a really quickly produced landscape is by using Edward Beal's "grassland" technique. This consists simply of dyeing several rolls of medical lint a good grass-green colour, and then tacking them in place over crumpled balls of newspaper to form grassy hills or railway embankments. The flock of the lint gives a surprisingly satisfactory representation of grass, and this method of "instant landscape" was used extensively at Craig in the early days. Later on, I used more conventional methods, working with Plaster of Paris or Alabastine filler over a foundation built up of odd strips of wood or card or anything else that happened to be handy—such as empty cardboard boxes. The general idea is

† Described in the "Railway Modeller" for March 1973.

* "Mountain, Moor, and Loch." Lond., 1894. 2nd ed. publ. by David & Charles, Newton Abbot, 1972.

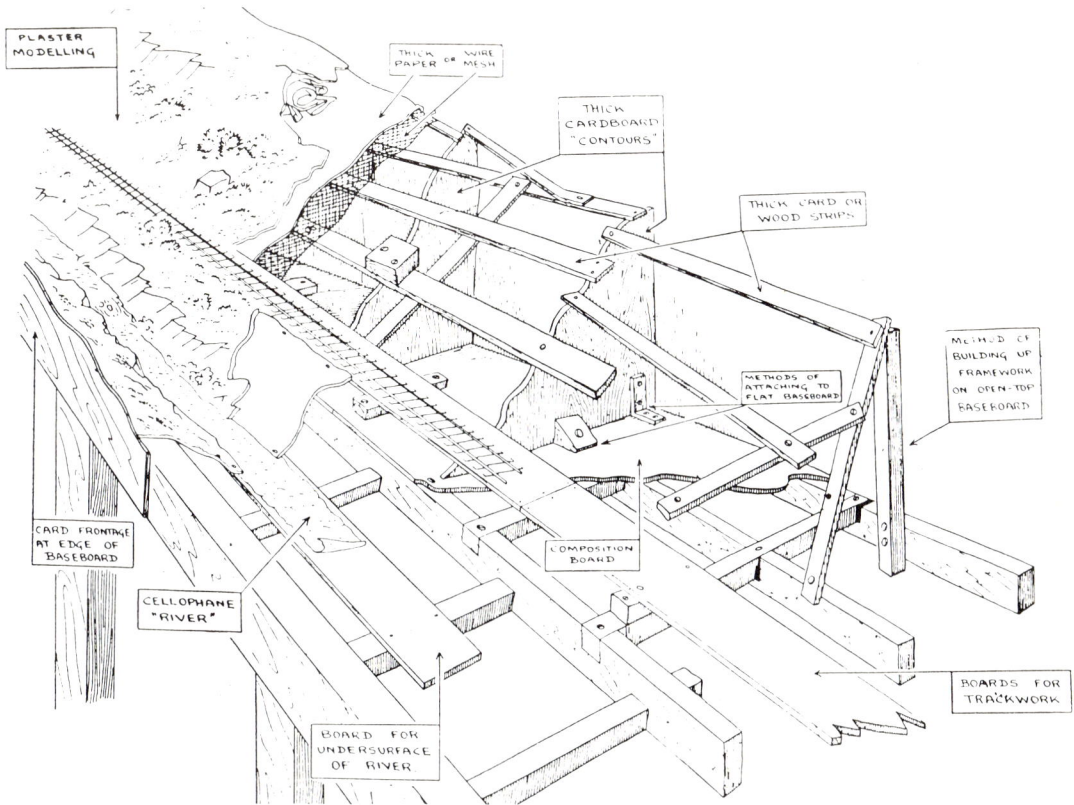

Landscape modelling with plaster of Paris or Polyfilla on a base of rough framework.

as shown in the accompanying drawing, and the technique which evolved was to cover the rough framework with several layers of wet newspaper and build up the plaster landscape on top of that. To the plaster was added a fair amount of sawdust and artist's powder colour. The sawdust was added partly to give a rough texture to the finished surface and partly to bind the plaster together ar.d prevent subsequent cracking or flaking. The powder colour, of course, imparted a built-in colour to the plaster mix, so that even if bits of the landscape did flake away the colour revealed was not the glaring white of untreated plaster. This might have been acceptable in a model landscape supposedly located in the chalk downs of the south of England, but would hardly have been appropriate for the mountains of Scotland.

All sorts of peculiar things have gone into the making of the Craigshire landscape, and when I am modelling a section of hill or railway cutting I work on a sort of intuitive basis, pressing pebbles, gravel, or pieces of cork bark into the still wet plaster to form rocky outcrops or scree slopes. I enjoy doing this sort of thing and feel slightly frustrated that I have never had room enough to get to work on a genuine model mountain of the sort which John Allen of Monterey in California managed to produce on his Gorre and Daphetid Railroad. I do have a few small burns trickling down my hills, but I hanker after some really torrential West Highland or Lake District style cascades with waterfalls toppling over drops of several hundred scale feet. One of my rivulets incorporates small pieces of broken ripple glass with the joints between each piece disguised as forming rapids. However, I have found that the most effective way of producing one of these rivulets is to model it in the plaster with a dry stream bed, such as might be found after a prolonged drought, complete with shingle, rocks, and undercut banks. I then pour clear varnish down the channel, wait for it to dry, and repeat the process ten, twenty, or even thirty times until quite a depth of "water" has been built up. Little pools tend to form naturally, and can be helped on their way while the varnish is still

At this stretch of the line the C.M.R. was lucky in being able to make use of an existing pack-horse bridge.

tacky. Waterfalls are allowed to take shape over lengths of polythene sheet fastened at the tops and bottoms of the falls. These falls, and also the little rapids which form around boulders, are painted with streaks and blobs of glossy white paint to represent foam. The only trouble is that dust and fluff do collect after a time in the water channels, and even if they are constantly removed, the original "wetness" of the water is eventually lost. The only thing for it then is to pour some more varnish down the channels and build up a new surface. Eventually, I suppose, the Craigshire burns and rivers will all overflow, and I shall have to set to work, dredge down to the original channels, and start all over again.

Another part of the landscape which is very difficult to keep fresh and clean is any afforestation. Trees, moreover, are notoriously difficult things to model satisfactorily in the first place. I think I must have tried all the conceivable methods of manufacture that there are, and yet Craigshire still remains

Here the West Water has been diverted into a culvert to make way for the standard-gauge track in the foreground. The water here consists of little pieces of green ripple glass.

comparatively unafforested. It is not merely the difficulty of making model trees which really look like trees, but of keeping them in good condition after they have been made. I have, in my time, made several model trees which I would almost dare to regard as genuine works of art, but, by the very nature of their perfection, these have been fragile things with gossamer-like foliage quite unfitted to withstand the rigours of everyday life on a model railway. Once made, they soon acquired a coating of dust and fluff which dulled their colours and clogged up the transparency of their foliage. Periodically this had to be blown away or sucked up with the vacuum cleaner, and in no time at all these autumnal breezes had whipped the branches bare and refoliation had to be carried out all over again.

In these circumstances it seemed not a bad idea to forget about foliage altogether, and to produce trees suitable for a winter landscape with no leaves at all, or else just a few straggling shreds and tatters. The only trouble here was that each tree, again, had to be really exceptionally well made to look realistic, since virtually every branch had to be modelled. The method I used was the well-tried one of using fairly thick cotton-covered wire for the main trunk and branches. This was twisted as shown in the accompanying drawing. Smaller clusters of branches were made from thinner enamel-coated wire, and these were wrapped around the ends of the larger branches and actually soldered into place where this seemed necessary. The division and further sub-division of the branches was taken several stages, and the models were finished with a couple of layers of paint and a few isolated patches of lichen and loofah foliage. They have stood up pretty well to the test of time, the only trouble being a tendency for the finer branches to become pushed out of shape when being dusted. I suppose that trees of this sort could be the eventual answer to Craigshire's afforestation problems, but they would never completely satisfy me, and I would always be hankering after trees in the full glory of summer or autumnal foliage. Thus only three of these fine-scale but wintry specimens have been made, and I have continued the search for other more quickly produced sorts of trees.

Spindly fir trees of the type often featured in the pages of the American "Model Railroader" can be made by inserting fronds of asparagus fern in holes drilled through trunks made from tapered dowel

rod or balsa wood. (Discarded "OO" paint brushes have a nice taper ready built into them.) The asparagus fern can be obtained from most good florists, but one has to beware, because it may be called

First attempts at tree modelling utilized bent wire for the trunks, and bathroom loofah for the foliage. Here are two early Scots pines, the first with a plastic wood, and the second with a Plasticine covering for the trunks.

At one time I thought that Britains Ltd. plastic model trees might be the answer to Craigshire's afforestation needs, but although the trees looked quite impressive when first planted, it was soon apparent that there was something not quite right about them, and they certainly did not come out well in photographs. This shot of "Hazeldean" near Dundreich was one of the slightly more satisfactory ones, but even so the over-scale leaves hit one in the eye straight away.

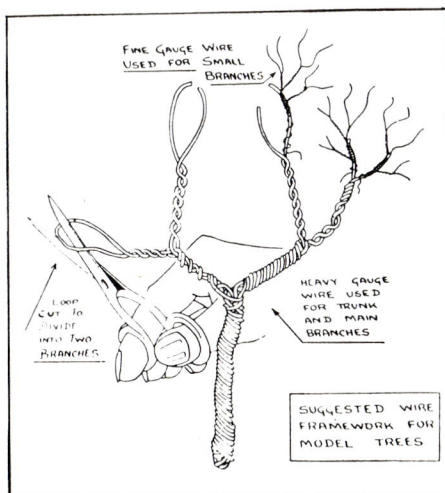

FINE GAUGE WIRE USED FOR SMALL BRANCHES

LOOP CUT TO DIVIDE INTO TWO BRANCHES

HEAVY GAUGE WIRE USED FOR TRUNK AND MAIN BRANCHES

SUGGESTED WIRE FRAMEWORK FOR MODEL TREES

maiden-hair fern—which it is not! Botanically-speaking what is wanted is Asparagus Plumosa—and if the "maiden-hair fern" offered by the florist looks like fine miniature ferns then this is what it probably is! The drawback to these trees lies, of course, in the delicacy of the fronds which are not easily dusted and which become brittle and faded after a year or two. However, the trees are undoubtedly easy to make and it does not take very long to remove the faded fronds and insert new ones in the trunks.

It is also possible to get Christmas-tree type fir trees made on the wire brush principle from Woolworths and other sources, and some of the model trees obtainable from Faller, Riko, Vollmer and other Continental firms are really quite effective in large massings, although they are expensive. At one time I had high hopes of the plastic trees produced by Britains Ltd. for use in their toy gardens. These provided the modeller with a nicely detailed tree trunk on to which clusters of plastic leaves could be clipped as desired. These leaf clusters actually had individual leaves of not too over-scale an appearance, and in theory it should have been possible to produce most realistic results. Indeed the trees did look fairly presentable when placed on the layout, but when they appeared in photographs they shrieked "model" at one straight away. Mind you, I think that there are very real possibilities here, and I can envisage some enterprising manufacturer eventually making available some really lace-like plastic leaf clusters. The nearest thing so far to what I have in mind is a plastic fern sold for use along with other plastic flowers as table decorations. This provides quite fine leaf clusters which can be clipped on to the ends of wire branches, and first experiments with the material are quite encouraging. It is not perhaps quite so fine a material as lichen or loofah, but it does have the great advantage of being stronger and longer lasting.

A final method of tree production which I have tried is that of using small sprigs of heather. This is an idea which has been suggested from time to time since the earliest days of small-scale railway modelling, but, with one or two notable exceptions, the results as illustrated by published photographs have not been very effective. This, perhaps, is because it has been assumed that any odd scraps of heather will do. Not a bit of it. I have come to the conclusion that the only really suitable heather grows in the furthest reaches of the Cheviots, or else in the most remote and inaccessible parts of the West Highlands, where the raging Atlantic storms have forced it to grow in suitable bent, tangled and gnarled positions. If one scrabbles around for a couple of hours on some west-facing sea cliffs one may be lucky enough to find one or two 4 mm scale miniature trees which only need paint-spraying and sawdust-leaf-sprinkling to reach the acme of perfection. In short, this is *not* the quick answer to tree production that it is sometimes claimed to be. So far, I have picked up about half a dozen of these heather beauties, and will no doubt get a few more as time goes on. An added difficulty in my case is that when I am in the West Highlands the last thing I am usually thinking about is searching for heather trees, and the possibility usually crosses my mind only when I am on the journey home.

Mention of natural materials for landscape modelling reminds me of "sea moss"—a fine fern like material which used to be sold at Woolworths, dyed a bright green colour, for use in some obscure hand craft. I have not seen this around for some time, which is a pity, because I am rather fond of it for small bushes or trackside weeds, and can spend hours fiddling about with bits and pieces to produce patches of riverside vegetation. Like all such materials it does not last for ever, but it does seem tougher than most, and some of the Craigshire trackside

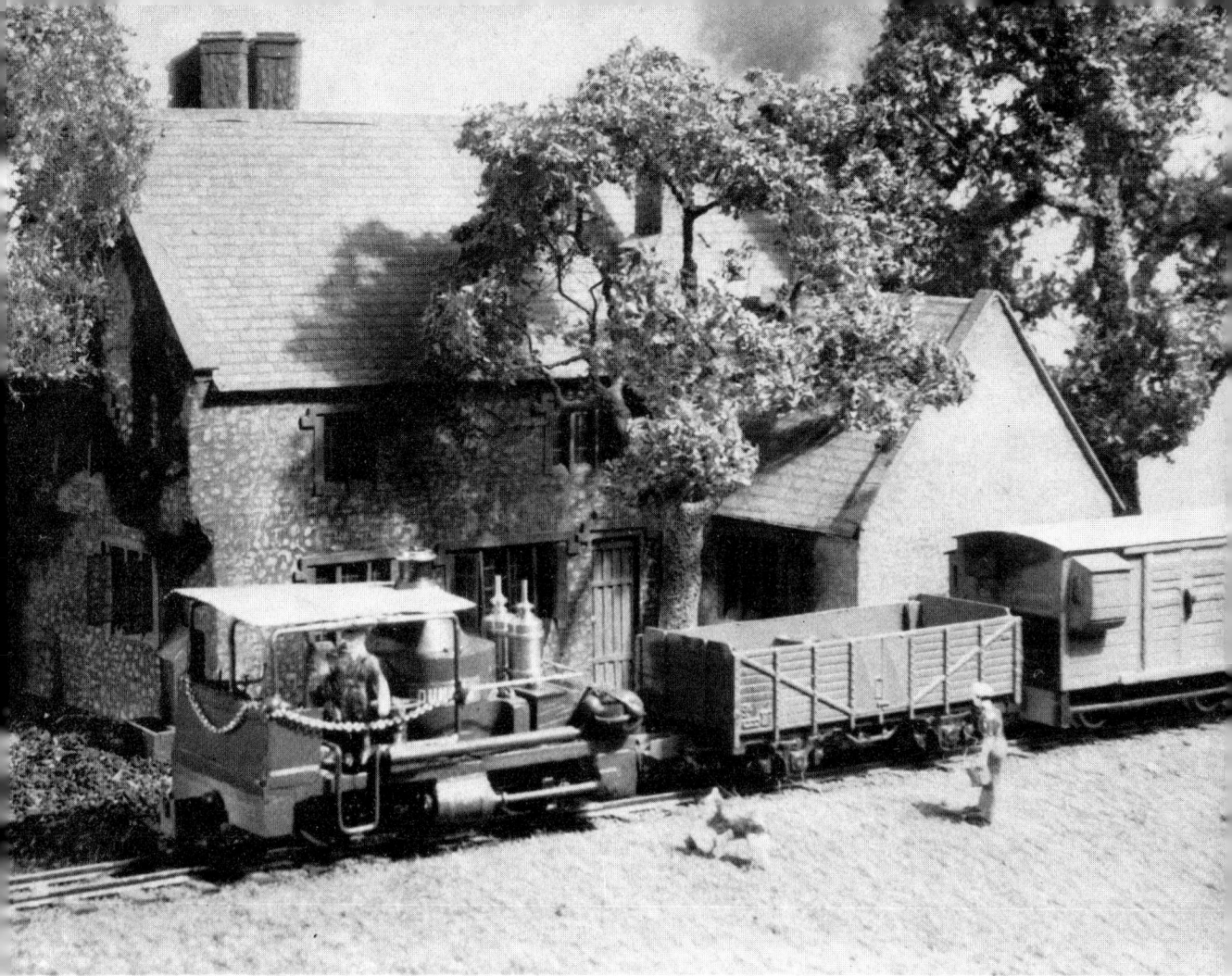

"Duncan" passing the Cotswold-type farm house in the early days of the layout. Two of the trees were examples of the meticulously modelled specimens at one time available from Bassett-Lowke Ltd.—perfect but fragile—and therefore destined to have only a comparatively short life. The grass on the embankment was made from a strip of green carpeting, which was an ideal material giving such excellent results that I cannot think why I did not experiment further with it.

weeds have been there now for well over a decade.

The provision of human and animal life at Craig is not nowadays the easy task it once was. The availability or non-availability of figures suitable for 4 mm scale layouts has passed through several stages in the past twenty-five years. In the days immediately after the war there was literally nothing at all, and for many years the production of miniature figures came very low down on the list of manufacturers' priorities —which was a matter of some surprise to me, since I could not conceive how any reasonably realistic layout could be built without them. I well remember how gratified I was when at long last I spotted an advertisement offering station staff and passengers for sale, and how disappointed I was when I received the mis-shapen, ill-painted blobs of lead which the manufacturer had had the temerity to call "perfect" miniatures. I returned them at once, suggesting that my money ought to be refunded, but, alas, that was

the last that I heard from that particular firm and I do not recollect seeing any more advertisements by it.

The first reasonably decent figures to appear on the market actually came via Ireland from a firm called "Authenticast." These were really "HO" gauge, or 3.5 mm scale figures, but were fairly generously proportioned and perfectly usable. Some of the characters acquired at this time are still to be seen in the Craigshire streets, notably a bevy o' girls in Tam o' Shanters waving hard after a perpetually departing train.

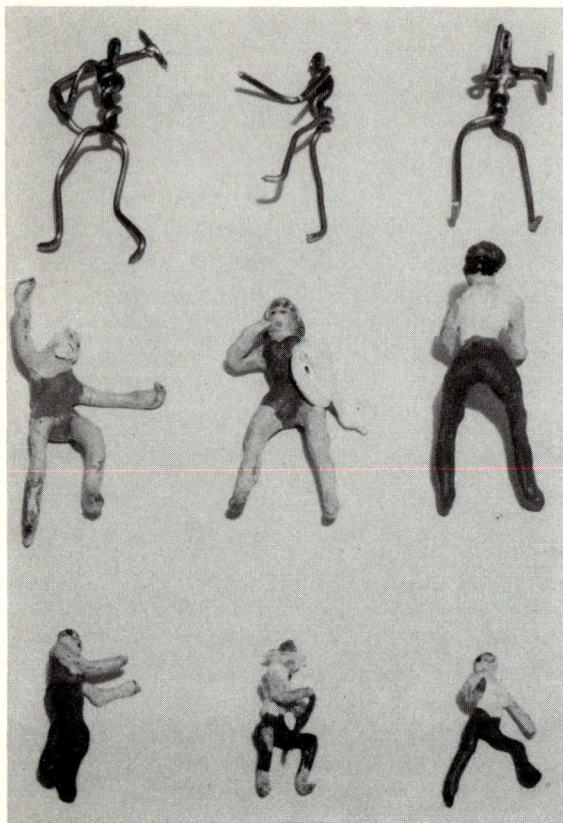

Wire frames, and examples of completed wax figures. The frames and top row of figures are to 7 mm scale, the bottom row to 4 mm scale.

The 'fifties were a good time for figures. First, there were the extremely good station staff and passenger sets from Graham Farish Ltd. These were actually over-scale for 4 mm, but this, of course, was all to the good when they were used alongside my 4.5 mm scale narrow-gauge models. I adopted the idea of using them in the foreground of the layout, and reserving the Authenticast and other figures for further back—a somewhat vague attempt at perspective modelling. Among these Graham Farish figures were several of real character. There was, for example, the rather stout gentleman designed for sprawling on a station seat in an attitude of relaxed, somnalent ease, his bowler hat tipped forward over his eyes. Another seated gentleman had one leg crossed nonchalently over the other while he scanned the sporting pages of the local newspaper. Similar well-animated figures were produced by the American firm of Weston— some of them even of semi-humorous nature. These figures sometimes had slightly unnatural proportions, but they could always be relied upon to be full of character and detail. Then there were Slater's plastic "huminiatures"—slightly flexible—and thus adaptable to a number of new poses. Hornby Dublo and Triang also produced a series of genuinely 4 mm scale figures, and I wish I had acquired more of these before they vanished from the scene. In fact I wish I had acquired more of these figures altogether since, with the inflow of Continental "HO" equipment,

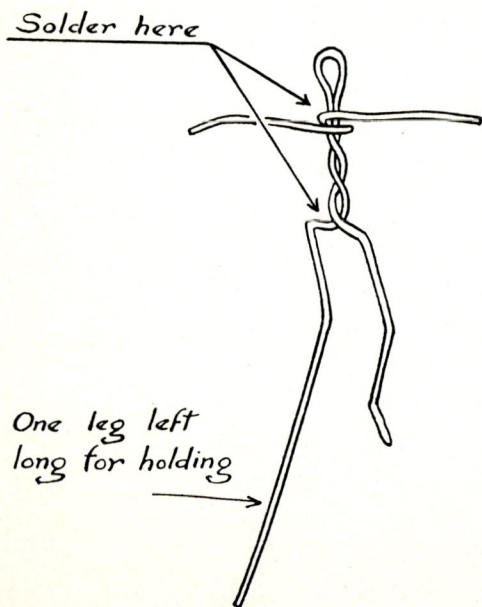

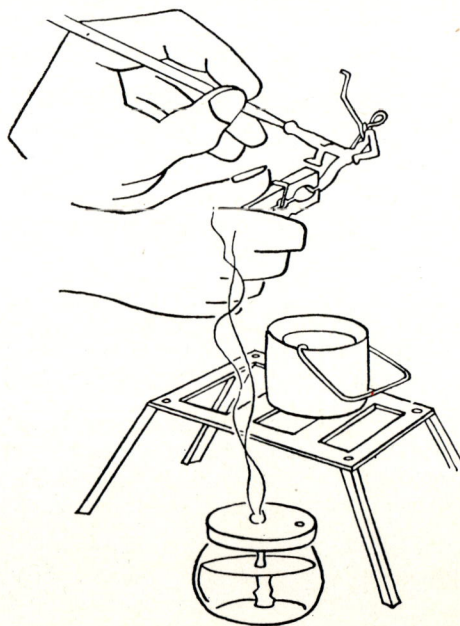

Solder here

One leg left long for holding

manufacturers have begun to produce figures theoretically suitable for both "HO" and "OO" gauge
layouts—which, of course, they cannot really be!
To make matters worse, many of the Continental
figures are nearer 3 mm than 3.5 mm scale, which
makes them even more unusable on a true 4 mm
scale layout, in spite of their exquisiteness as models.
Indeed, one of the few sources of genuinely 4 mm
scale figures nowadays would seem to be from the
world of model soldiers, where several of the types
of "20 mm" war-game figures are fairly easily adapted
to civilian needs.

*Glenmuir's oldest inhabitant is Davie Gilmore, made from
wax brushed on to a wire framework, and with a paper
washer acting as the brim of his floppy hat. The C.M.R.
track is super-detailed here but does, I must admit, look
horribly overscale. Peco small-section rail was simply not yet
available when Glenmuir was built.*

*A selection of Graham Farish standing and seated passenger
figures on the platform at Craig. "Agnes" with goods train
in the background.*

It is also possible to make wax figures by brushing
hot wax on to suitably prepared wire frames. I tried
this when I wanted some special pre-Grouping
figures, and found it quite interesting. The biggest
difficulty proved to be that of obtaining suitable
modelling wax. Somehow I never thought of a
Chemist's shop, where it is possible to obtain slabs
of beeswax, which would probably be ideal. Instead,
after trying every other conceivable source, I ended
up at a shop supplying Church furniture and equipment and, after having been assured that it would

*One of the wax figures at work with hammer on the track
at Glenmuir. The figure with the oil lamps in the background
is one of the Graham Farish metal figures.*

Slater's plastic "huminiatures" on the horse-drawn coal flat, and Authenticast metal figures around "Duncan." The excellent plastic horse is another Slater's production.

Graham Farish locomen surrounding "Kettledrummle" as she rolls slowly off the turntable towards the coaling stage. These metal figures had plenty of character and were much closer to true 4 mm scale than most commercial figures which try to get the best of both worlds by being a bit on the small side and calling themselves "HO/OO" scale!

not be regarded in any way as sacrilege, bought myself half a pound of broken altar candles which were made of the very best quality wax, and which proved to be excellent for the purpose required. I found it best to heat the wax in a small dish over a spirit lamp, and to brush it on to the wire frames while it was still liquid but not too hot. Several layers could be built up quite quickly, and although the finished figures lacked the detail of quality castings they made up for it by liveliness of posture, and a multitude of sins could be covered by careful attention to the final paint work.

One minor point about figures that might be worth mentioning is that I always remove the bases from any commercial figures before fixing them in place on the layout. All too often when one is looking at

model railway photographs one finds that any chance of mistaking them for the real thing is destroyed by the obtrusive bases attached to the human figures. No doubt the bases are useful if the figures are constantly being moved from one part of the layout to another, but in Craigshire, at any rate, most of the figures are an integral part of the scenes in which they appear, and are stuck in place on the baseboard with a couple of dabs of polystyrene cement on the soles of their feet if they are made of plastic, or of Durofix or Uhu if they are metal. Half a dozen or so "special" figures do move around (largely for photographic purposes) but even these have no bases and are simply positioned carefully as required—sometimes leaning against a building or locomotive—or even, if I don't breathe too hard on them—managing to stand erect and well balanced on their miniscule feet!

Nowadays there are quite a large number of plastic building kits available, but, apart from those produced by Airfix Ltd., most of them are of Continental or American design. I have, however, found them a most useful source of spare parts, and have long

A variety of commercial figures at Craig station, all re-dressed in period costume to fit the pre-Grouping scene.

Hotel porters collecting luggage from Craig station. These are Weston metal figures, manufactured in the U.S.

Cotswold-style house. This was the very first building I made for the layout, and it is still part of the Craigshire landscape, although it has long since been deposed from its original place of honour on the top of Craig Hill. The stonework was achieved by using pieces of finely embossed wallpaper as a building paper. The effect was quite pleasing, although perhaps a trifle too regular.

since given up scribing window sashes on celluloid or acetate sheet, since the plastic windows from kits are so very good. One building kit of which I have made especially good use is the old-fashioned factory building produced by Vollmer. This actually does fit very well into a British townscape, and the windows are ideal for many purposes. Some of them are half-rounded at the top, and these are just what are required for Georgian buildings.

Most of Craigshire's buildings, however, are made from cardboard—either two thicknesses of Bristol Board—or else one thickness of photographic mounting board. The thicker board is really the better for stone-built Scottish buildings with deeply inset windows, but I used to fight shy of it because of the difficulty of getting really sharp corners when cutting out window openings with a razor-blade. Now I use one of the very convenient Swann-Morton craft knives, and the sharp-pointed blade which this uses has converted the frustration of cutting out windows into a pleasure.

I usually cut out each wall of a building separately,

and, when sticking them together, reinforce each corner internally with lengths of stripwood. I have used all sorts of glues over the years, from Seccotine and balsa cement to Uhu and Bostik, but I am becoming fonder and fonder of white-paste wood-working adhesive—largely because it does not have the strong smell of the other glues—a somewhat important point when my workshop is also my bedroom! Unfortunately, this white-paste glue does not seem to be all that easy to get hold of. Different manufacturers have produced it over the years and then abandoned it, but at the time of writing it is available in the Evo-stik range of adhesives.

There are far more brick-built buildings in Scotland

Close-up details of stonework and windows of the Cotswold house.

nowadays than there were fifty years ago, but they are usually disguised by harling, stucco, or pebble-dash finishes, and only factory or older railway buildings blatantly display their brickwork. Most of Scotland still gives the impression of being a land of stone-built houses, and many of the buildings in the main streets of Scottish towns are of close-fitting granite blocks. I have found that the easiest way to represent these is simply to draw them in with pencil, or with pen and ink, on the actual walls of the buildings being modelled. This can be done quite quickly and is a method with definite advantages since there is no difficulty in obtaining whatever sort of fancy stonework may be required, and the stone facings around windows can all be drawn in properly. When brick-built buildings have been required I have, from time to time, been able to make use of embossed building cards produced by a variety of manufacturers, but I still have a partiality for the old-fashioned Merco and Modelcraft brick papers. Applying these papers to the outside of a model building, however, is not quite as easy as it looks. If the window openings are pre-cut to match

those in the building it may be found that they will cease to match once paste has been applied to the paper, since the paste will make it stretch slightly. If some form of glue is used instead of paste this may form little streaks behind the building paper, and these can show through in a most displeasing way. So—although it is cheating in a way—what I usually do is to pre-paste the paper to stretch it, and then I apply it to the side of the building in one unbroken layer. After it is dry I cut through the paper which is covering each window opening—either to an "X" or an "H" pattern—and bend the little panels so formed back into the building, where they are pasted to the inside walls.

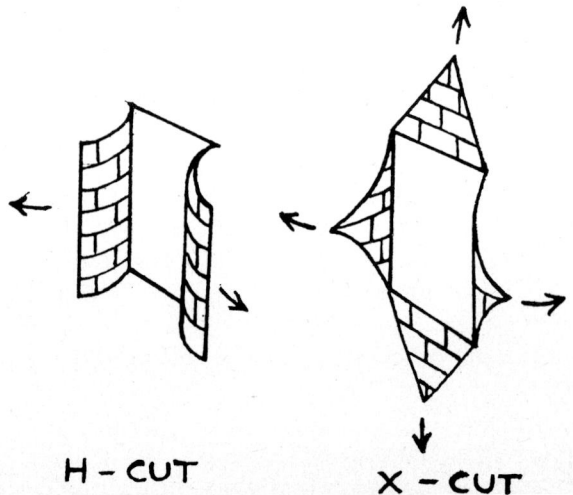

H - CUT   X - CUT

There have always been a good many fences and railings in Craig. These are especially appropriate in a pre-Grouping townscape, since they help to create that sense of unity and coherence which is rapidly being lost in towns today. Few houses or public buildings are given well-designed railings nowadays, and town planners are especially fond of "informal" open areas and flower plots which look fine in architectural drawings but which, in actual practice, rapidly degenerate into bare trodden earth and rubbish dumps. Moreover, the railings or fences which house owners, in desperation, erect around their own homes, do little to add coherence to a street, since they are all different, and some are little more than metal poles and wire mesh!

How different in the old days when even the humblest "slum" tenement had its solid Victorian railings protecting the miniscule gardens, whilst more imposing houses and public buildings could boast the most elaborate wrought ironwork designs. Alas, most of these were swept away in 1941 or 1942 as part of the War Effort—a useless sacrifice as it so turned out, since it was discovered too late that most of the iron was quite unsuitable for the forging of modern weapons of war—and many of the railings simply rusted away where they had been dumped.

Fishermen's cottages on Craig waterfront. This is a model of Sailor's Walk, Kirkcaldy. The taller, gable-ended building on the right is now owned by the National Trust, but the smaller cottages have now been demolished—a pity, because it was their outside stairways and the roofs sloping at various angles which contributed so greatly to the character of the whole group. My own model is not really as well made as I should like and I fear that the Merco old-stone building paper does not give quite the correct effect. I have a suspicion, moreover, that my model is grossly overscale, so one day I must make a special visit to Kirkcaldy to measure the National Trust property on the spot, and then build a much better model. There is, incidentally, an excellent photograph of the group as it was in Robert Hurd's book, "Scotland Under Trust."

No doubt if I had the time for it, I could create some really ornate railings for parts of Craig, but I am afraid that I have always taken the easy way out and made use of whatever commercial products were available. Most of the plastic fences available are representations of railway paling or of country wooden fences. However I do have a yard or two of cast metal railing (maker unknown) which is not too unlike the traditional Victorian railing. Britain's Ltd. produce a beautifully ornate "wrought-iron" gate, made of plastic, as part of their garden series, and a number of these can be adapted or joined together to suit quite a variety of circumstances—the only difficulty being that the plastic they are made of is

The backs of the buildings opposite show that what the eye does not see the heart does not grieve over! The buildings are designed to be placed flat against the wall of the room, so there is really little point in providing them with backs.

of that particularly unglue-able sort of polythene. Some of the Vollmer kits yield very presentable little bits of railing, but as far as I know these are not available separately. In fact the field seems to be wide open for some enterprising manufacturer as far as railings are concerned. Would they be too fragile in white metal, I wonder?

I think the thing which has caused me most trouble in modelling the Craigshire landscape has simply been the difficulty inherent in trying to create a harmonious picture with no incongruities or ana-chronisms. I realize, of course, that a landscape does not need to be harmonious or pleasant to look at in order to be realistic. Indeed it would often seem to be the desire of present day planners to make our towns and countryside as ugly and dispiriting as possible. A model of some of the incoherent hotch-potches of architectural style which now disfigure so many of our towns would no doubt be realistic enough, but it certainly would not please me, and would not be the sort of "picture in three dimensions" which I am trying to create at Craig.

Even today—where one can find a small town or

village which has not been too developed—it is amazing how often the older central area seems to fit together like a glove, and how each building seems to harmonize with its neighbours—in marked contrast to the more modern, outlying areas which, all too often, give one that feeling of just not belonging. Of course, builders and architects of a hundred years and more ago were still working with traditional materials such as stone, brick, timber or tile, and these were bound to blend together better than ferro-concrete and steel. Nevertheless it is surprising what an instinctive feel they seemed to have for the well planned street or town square, and how often they managed to arrange for a pleasing view at each road end. Today there is much conscious town planning and talk in the textbooks about these things, but somehow the results never seem to be so happy as they used to be when they just happened by that mixture of chance and instinct which went together for so long to create the traditional British town and village in the traditional British landscape.

Mind you, it is certainly not easy when placing model buildings next to each other to say just why some seem to fit together naturally and pleasantly while others simply look wrong. It is not a matter merely of different building styles, different sizes of window, or even different heights of floor, since sometimes the contrast provided between a low-storeyed

Group of houses in the main street, Craig. These are based upon some rather pleasant buildings in Haddington, and are quite good examples of the "traditional" cardboard and building-paper methods of construction in vogue before plastic building kits and styrene sheet became available. Even today the results so easily obtained by using building-papers are not to be despised.

mediaeval house and a Georgian villa actually helps to create a picturesque grouping. As I say, a great deal seems to depend simply upon a strange intuitive "feel" for things, and in me this seems to be only half developed. However, in arranging the background row of houses at Craig I have found that things have become easier as I have accumulated more buildings, since it has been possible to try out different arrangements and to keep juggling things around until finally I have reached something which continues to look fairly satisfactory to me. A study of the photographs in this book reveals only too clearly the roving careers of some of Craigshire's buildings. The fishermen's cottages, for example, have in their time moved from one end of Craig to the other, and the "Cotswold-type" farmhouse now at the foot of Craighill was once actually perched on the top.

I have to confess that the actual standards of modelling achieved at Craig are not as high as I should like, and probably not as high even as those which I could achieve if I were to exert myself really very hard. In some respects, indeed, the standard of individual models may actually have fallen since the early days, since it did not take me very long to discover that if I were to continue as painstakingly as I had begun I would never have a complete model railway layout, but only a collection

of isolated models—pleasing enough in themselves—but not what I really wanted. Moreover, with the time actually available for modelling being so limited, there has always been some difficulty in maintaining the initial enthusiasm with which each model has been started. Some models have been started, put aside for some months, picked up again, nibbled at, and not finally completed until years later. In these circumstances I have always been very loath to scrap work already done, and this is why each version of Craigshire has leant so heavily upon its predecessor. On several occasions I have been tempted to start afresh on entirely new lines—perhaps even in an entirely new scale—but I have always been brought back to earth by remembering the length of time which it has already taken for Craigshire to reach its present state. So, whether I like it or not, I have been forced to remain true to my original vision, and have managed to obtain a great deal of satisfaction out of Craigshire's slow development. It has not at all been a straightforward progression from an

Craig waterfront before the trams came really did have something of an air of old-world peacefulness about it. However, as Mr. Tom Smallways said, "This here Progress—it keeps on." The only consolation is that Progress in Craigshire is not so irrevocably one-way as in the larger world outside. It is quite within the bounds of probability, for example, that Craig Town Council will decide to pull down a few fairly modern-looking buildings and replace them with something far more antiquated and picturesque.

early simple layout to a more complex and more "perfect" one. In fact, the increasing complexity of the layout sometimes meant periods of considerable decline in its overall effectiveness, and much fiddling and messing about has been necessary before I could become satisfied with each new development. Even then there would remain regrets at the passing of certain pleasing features which had had to be discarded in order to make room for those new developments, and the next stage would therefore see the slow dawning of new ideas designed to recover something of what had been lost. Thus it has been one step back for every two forward, and there has never been a time when I could say, "this is it—the layout is finished!"

I suppose that what I have really been trying to do all these years is to fit a model railway into an "ideal" landscape. Craig, I suppose, is the kind of little town I would be quite pleased to live in, while the little bit of Craigshire countryside which is all that is

visible from the railway stretches on in my imagination into the Craigshire Highlands, which are a curious amalgam of all that is best in the Scottish Highlands, the Border Country, and the English Lake District. Set in the heart of this mountainous countryside, nestling between Dundreich and Carn Liath hills, and overlooking a pleasant loch which looks something like parts of Coniston Water, lies the little village of Mertonford, which has hardly been mentioned in the course of this book, in spite of its being the professed reason for the existence of the C.M.R. I do not know myself what Mertonford looks like. Obviously it is something rather special, but I don't think I shall ever try to build a model of the place. It is the ultimate unobtainable goal towards which it is always better to travel hopefully than to arrive. Perhaps one day I shall be allowed a glimpse of it, but, in the meantime, much remains to be done. As I have already mentioned, the second stage of Craigshire's history is already drawing to a close and once again the pattern of dismantling and rebuilding is to be repeated. On the whole, I think that the first forced dismantling turned out to be a blessing in disguise, and that the second Craigshire was really better than the first. Of course, it could have been even better—so now I am touching wood and hoping that the third Craigshire will not only recover some of the lost virtues of the first, but will also move onward to new and better things. Time alone will show whether or not my hopes are justified.

12 Recent Developments

Since the first publication of this book the third layout, envisaged in the previous chapter, has begun to take shape, and it seems appropriate to add a short postscript to bring the story more up to date. The second enforced redecoration of my bedroom gave the necessary impetus to do something about the increasing dissatisfaction which I had begun to feel about certain features of the second layout. In particular I regretted the absence of the harbour which had been such an important focal point of the first layout. It had vanished simply because there no longer seemed to be any room for it. The expansion of my interests to include standard gauge and tramway modelling as well as narrow gauge modelling meant that the layout had to have much more trackwork—or, at least, that's what I thought then. I had therefore crammed a combined standard and narrow gauge station into the space once occupied by the harbour and was sorry ever afterwards. It not only looked too crowded, but it turned out when I came to operate the layout that the main line trains were too long for the station anyway, and that the major operational interest developed into the marshalling and operating of goods trains according to the card system described in Chapter 7.

It slowly dawned upon me that the large passenger station was rather wasted, and eventually I realised that there was no actual rule which said that it was compulsory to have a passenger station as part of a model railway layout! I began to think of the possibility of a layout in which the continuous run would exist mainly as the means whereby impressive main line trains could show off their paces without actually going anywhere except back to their storage sidings, and where the operational interest would, as before, centre upon the goods train operation. If Craig were to consist mainly of goods sidings then why could not these be situated picturesquely around a revived Craig harbour? Of course, there would have to be provision for the narrow gauge C.M.R. and this could be attractively provided for by a small pier station actually projecting into the harbour, thus providing a fine opportunity for some interesting scenic modelling.

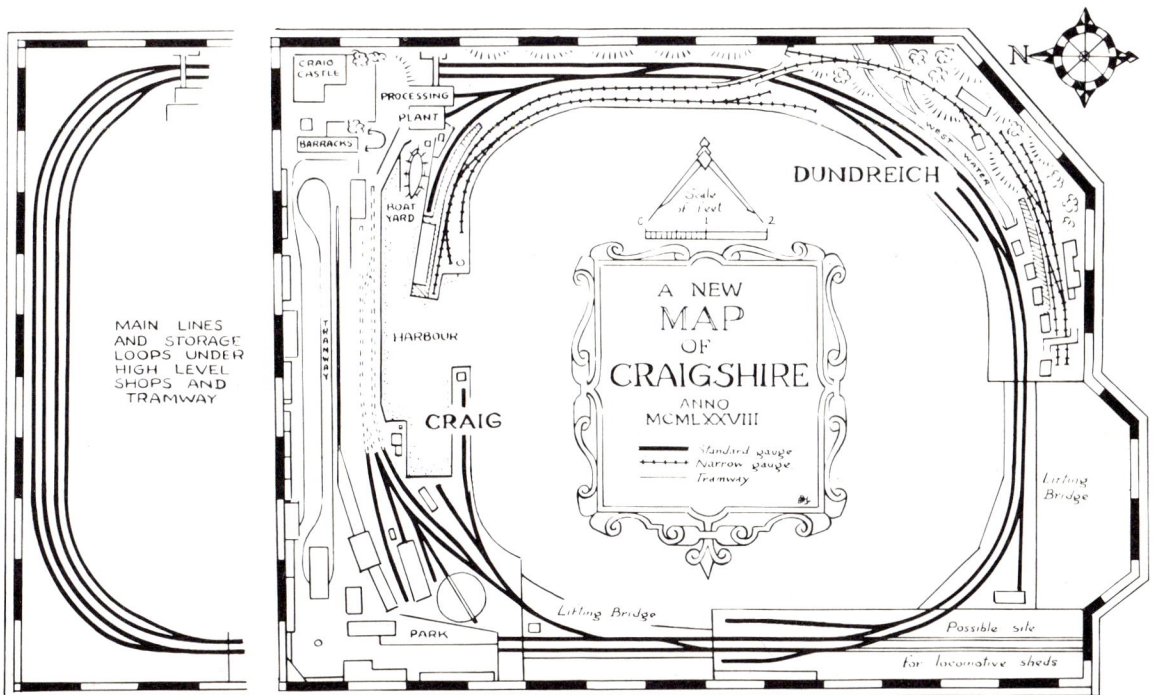

The border of the map is divided in feet.

Sometimes when I think of bright ideas like this they tarnish very rapidly, but this one still seemed quite good a couple of years after I first thought of it, so when the time came to start work upon my third layout the new harbour was the very first consideration, and it is now the first part of the layout in a reasonably complete state. It has not, of course, been a case of complete rebuilding since as many as possible of the buildings and other features of the old layouts have been preserved and incorporated into the new. Nevertheless, a surprising number of new buildings have had to be made.

Pride of place is taken by the large warehouse of the Craig Storage Co. which is concocted from a mixture of Heljan and Vollmer plastic factory parts, and is the largest building yet constructed for Craigshire. More than half the background buildings in Harbour Street are new, and more typically Scottish than the older ones which had to be replaced anyway because of increasing decrepitude. Craig church is a much more glorious structure than it used to be, and even boasts one of those musical-box sets of bell chimes that came with the Triang church of some years ago. A couple of doors down from the church—to the great annoyance of the Minister—is Craig's new centre of entertainment—the Alhambra Theatre. This, as can be seen from one of the photographs, is now showing 'The Quaker Girl'—Lionel Monckton's new production straight from its successful run in nearby Edinburgh—which shows that the third layout still tries to pin Craigshire down to a date of around 1912, even though I am still toying with the idea of moving things into the nineteen-twenties. Indeed, the latest N.B. locos have actually been painted in the immediate pre-Grouping style, with numbers between the 'N' and the 'B' on tenders or side tanks. There is even one of the new Hornby J. 83 0-6-OT locomotives which is still in L.N.E.R. livery. I am obviously trying to get the best of both worlds, with some stock finished in the 'new' Grouping liveries, but with the majority of locomotives and coaches still in the old liveries. If this continues I will obviously have to convert the Alhambra into one of those new-fangled moving picture palaces, and change the week's attraction to Rudolph Valentino in 'The Four Horsemen of the Apocalypse'.

I found that one of the greatest difficulties in rebuilding Craigshire was the way in which things which worked perfectly on the old layout ceased to work when they were incorporated in the new. Trackwork which never caused any trouble before was found to be strangely out of gauge when re-assembled; locomotives which were in perfect working order when packed away in their boxes had developed mysterious short circuits by the time they were once more brought into the light of day; wagon wheels had accumulated extra layers of dirt purely by magnetic or capillary attraction or something. It was all most mysterious. There is now, for example, an amazing spot where the gradient on the narrow gauge line out of Craig eases up and where the track is now level for a few inches. Here trains now sometimes uncouple accidentally from their locomotives, which then have to chase furiously back after the coaches as they hurtle back to the Pier station. It was this feature which gave me the idea for the ultra simple space-saving track formation on the Pier—no run-round—merely a length of track with a siding. The idea was that if the trains would insist upon uncoupling at that particular point on the gradient we might as well let a train coming from Dundreich (see plan) uncouple there on purpose. The coaches would be held by some means or another on the gradient, while the

Craig harbour looking west, the scene dominated by the warehouses of the Craig Storage Company, behind which is situated the small tram depot.

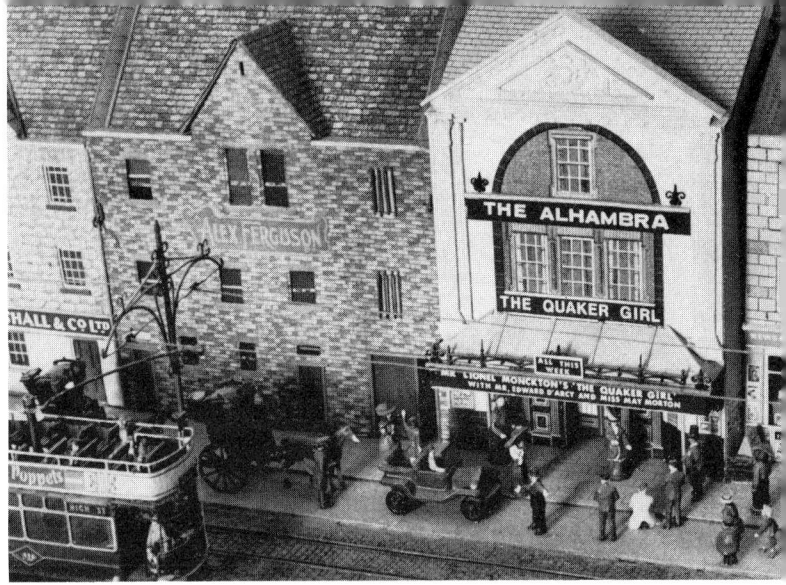

Close up of the Alhambra Theatre in Harbour Street. Note the hansom cabs awaiting custom. These are made from a little plastic kit which was obtainable from Woolworths many years ago— probably made in Hong Kong.

locomotive would carry on to the Pier and move into the siding. The coaches would then be allowed to rumble on into the station by their own volition, past the entrance to the siding in which the locomotive was parked all ready to move out, and couple on to the front of the train again when required. Unfortunately when it came to put this idea into practice it was discovered that there were great difficulties involved in getting the same degree of 'rollability' into all vehicles. It was also discovered that an awkwardly sharp curve had been built into the track just outside the station and 'Alistair' had trouble getting round this. All sorts of things were done to get over this, including the cutting away of parts of 'Alistair's' confining outside frames in order to give more play to the pony trucks. This enabled 'Alistair' to get round the curve, but the locomotive's overall length meant that the couplings still stuck far out over the curve and tended to pull vehicles off the track! This was a brand new sort of problem caused by the fact that the C.M.R.'s couplings have now been changed from the Triang/Hornby type— which had plenty of room for the coupling hook to slide about in—to the more compact Eggerbahn type which look neater but, as I now discover, have their own problems. I am afraid that the answer here is that the track is just going to have to be relaid in order to ease the curve, and when this is done I think I will also settle for a conventional run-round and squeeze it in somehow or other. It just doesn't pay to try to be too clever!

In fact as far as operation is concerned I have long since decided that the simpler things are better as far as Craigshire is concerned. As described in Chapter 7, the standard gauge track used to be split up into eight sections, now it is only four—two for the up line and two for the down. There are two controllers, each of which can operate the whole of the standard gauge if all the sections are switched into it, but normally the two sections for the up line are connected to one controller and the two for the down line to the other. The narrow gauge C.M.R. is all one section, and it can be operated either from a controller at Craig or from one at Dundreich. All points are still manually operated by hand levers at the side of the track. On my first layout I had electrically operated points, and the manually operated ones on the second layout were meant to be only temporary. Like so many temporary things, however, they went on and on, and I have a funny feeling that the manual levers on my new layout may also be destined for a long life. I suppose I should object to the intrusion of my great over-scale hand to operate the points, but I find that it offends my aesthetic sense as little as does the intrusion of an over-scale uncoupling pole to deal with the three-link couplings on the standard gauge wagons. In fact I have a suspicion that I like having something to do apart from turning controller knobs and pressing buttons.

I suppose another example of my laziness is the way in which for many years I have dodged the problem of signals on the layout. I have always had a few signals just for atmosphere, but have never made any attempt to signal the layout properly. This was partly due to a certain lack of interest in railway signals as such, and partly due to the difficulty in making proper lattice-post N.B.R. signals. I did try the experiment of using perspex for a signal post and

Craig parish church—a model based upon Newington Parish Church in Edinburgh.

painting the lattice work thereon. This was quite effective as long as the perspex remained transparent, and the deception actually fooled quite a number of people. However, the passage of a few years soon dimmed the transparency of the post to a most distressing degree, and I am glad I never put the idea into mass production. Then a few years ago Ratio brought out their lattice post L.N.E. signals and, although these are of a heavier section than true-scale N.B. posts would be, I have nevertheless managed to use them to produce quite presentable models, with the very distinctive N.B. type of signal arm cut from brass sheet and painted appropriately. Gradually these are being installed in the proper positions on the layout—at least on the main line—although older 'Craigshire Northern Railway' wooden post signals are being allowed to remain elsewhere. All the signals

are still purely decorative, but hope springs eternal in the human breast, and one of these days I may get around to connecting them up to the pointwork.

Another thing which the passage of time has dulled is the coloured photographic posters which I produced a good many years ago for the first pre-Grouping layout. These have had to be replaced by new prints and are now supplemented by a selection from the new 'Tiny Signs' and Pendon-produced posters.

When I first became interested in railway modelling it seemed hard to believe that the day could ever come when I would have more rolling stock than my layout could actually hold. However locomotives, wagons and coaches do accumulate in a remarkable way, and while things were in the interregnum state between layouts I conducted a ruthless blitz upon Craigshire's equipment and disposed of most of my more modern interlopers—things like A3 pacifics or d.m.u.s, and also all coaches and wagons which failed to meet required standards. Some of this stuff was sold privately, some given away, and some sold to several of those firms which advertise for your unwanted equipment and offer 'best prices'. Upon reflection, I would probably have done much better simply had I cannibalised some of the unwanted equipment for motors, wheels and other parts since, in most instances, the 'best prices' received hardly made it worth-while parcelling the equipment up and posting it off. However, the exercise did clear the decks for a while—even if only for a while—because stock is now beginning to accumulate again—especially in the locomotive field, since manufacturers are continuing to produce an almost embarrassing number of kits for locomotives which fit perfectly into my pre-Grouping scene—embarrassing because I am in two minds about the virtues of white metal kits. I find that it takes *almost* as long to assemble one of them properly as to build a model from scratch, and at the end of the day I have something which I can never call entirely my own. It may be—probably will be—a much more accurate model than I could build myself, and yet it remains 'only' a kit, and somehow this takes part of the savour away.

On the other hand, white metal kits do have the positive virtue of built-in weight, which is invaluable for the improvement both of hauling capacity and current pickup—and anyway, I just can't resist buying them. I have, by now, evolved my own patent methods of assembling them. This involves soldering together the main boiler parts and any other parts which provide enough thickness of metal to enable soldering to be carried out with a reasonable degree of safety. This provides a basic shell to which the smaller, more delicate parts can be attached by epoxy or cyanoacrylic glues (some of which scare me), plastic padding (which I rather like) or even good old durofix. I find that the soft nickel silver wire which is usually provided for handrails soon gets bent and kinked, and I usually replace this by thin piano wire which, being steel, looks better anyway. I also substitute W. & H.'s brass handrail knobs for the split pin variety provided in the kits. I am aware that these brass handrail knobs are really over scale, and that in many respects the split pins almost do a better job, but I sometimes find difficulty in keeping the handrails the proper distance away from the boiler when using the split pins, and somehow the turned brass knobs just look better to me. I have, on occasion, used true 'dead-to-scale' handrail knobs, but these take handrail wire which has to be almost too thin, and

they are horribly fragile and easily broken . . . one has to make *some* compromises in small scale railway modelling—at least I do.

Before painting any completed white metal model I burnish it with an old, rather stiff, hogs-hair paintbrush to remove as far as possible any file marks and scratches. I then give a thinned down coat of Humbrol chromate primer, and a few days later I say a prayer and begin painting. I suppose I ought to try to move with the times and master the art of spray painting. I have tried, but with indifferent results, and still feel much happier with a paintbrush in my hand. Then again, I gather that when painting by hand the best results are obtained by applying two or three very thin coats, but I can never do this without getting small bubbles or streaks in the paint, and so I have to confess that I try to get the body colour on in one go, using paint thinned down slightly from the consistency as supplied in the tin, and trying to brush it on so that it flows naturally into place. Sometimes I suceed; sometimes I don't. The great secret seems to be that I just have to be in the right mood for painting. A sort of sixth sense tells me when it is time to drop everything else and get out the paintbrushes; if I try at any

Craig harbour looking east.

View of "Glen Roy". The track in the foreground does not mean that we are moving over to a three-rail system of electrification! This is a stretch of track at one time intended for dual-gauge operation.

other time disaster is almost inevitable. If disaster does strike and I end up with a hopeless paint job it is always possible to use paint remover and scrapers and strip the paint off a white metal or brass model and try again—and I am told that it is even possible successfully to remove paint from a plastic model by means of the judicious application of motor car brake fluid (the used variety is quite suitable!)

Some of the photographs illustrating this chapter show the two white metal locomotives most recently added to the stock. These are N.B.R. 0-6-0 C class, no. 47, and 4-4-0 K class 'Glen Roy'. The 0-6-0 has a home made chassis, Stewart-Reidpath driving wheels and an old American Mantua motor which is very good but unfortunately sticks rather far back into the cab. This is a feature which would have horrified me in my early, more perfectionist years but which, I fear, I am nowadays inclined to let slip by in the interests of operational efficiency. I could—and should, of course—try to remount the motor less obtrusively, but at the moment the locomotive works well, and once I have got an engine working my golden rule is to leave well alone because, if I start messing about with it, I'm sure to end up with a model which

may look better, but which never works properly again.

One feature of interest about the mechanism is the incorporation of a 'delayed action' drive—a feature described by K. N. McAldowie in the old 'Model Railway News' as long ago as August 1948 and which I have always wanted to try. The idea is very simple. The worm wheel is not fixed on to the driving axle but is allowed to revolve freely between washers which keep it centrally located on the axle. It carries a small, projecting steel peg, and this engages with a similar

"Alistair"—the pride of the narrow-gauge Craig and Mertonford Light Railway. The model was built nearly 25 years ago—by H. B. Whall and Cherrys Ltd., and is of one of the Manning-Wardle 2-6-2T's which used to run on the late lamented Lynton and Barnstaple Railway. This photograph shows "Alistair" in the C.M.R.'s older dark green livery.

peg projecting from the axle. The little diagram should make things clear. It means that the gears always have a certain amount of travel before the pegs engage, thus giving the electric motor a chance to get going before taking up the load. When current is cut off, the worm wheel will still revolve a bit, allowing a certain amount of coasting to take place. Thus if current collection is impaired by a length of dirty track, for example, the locomotive will not be halted but will glide over the dirty bits. Anyway, that's the theory, and I *think* it works! When starting, the motor also invariably revolves free for a while, then there is a slight jerk as the load is taken up, and away we glide! The only trouble is that one has to evolve a special driving technique for this particular locomotive, and its behaviour can be a little disconcerting until one becomes used to it.

This is all part of the search for improved current collection and better running qualities. In this quest I have pursued any and every will o' the wisp as it has come up in the model railway press over the years. Flywheels, sprung wheel suspensions, direct rail contacts, and now this little gimmick. Some, however —such as wheel springing—turn out, in my hands at least, to be bristling with hidden gremlins. I've tried 'em all and, while they all help, nothing alters the fact that a layout in a bedroom accumulates an awful lot of dust and fluff, and nothing is going to operate at all until that is vacuumed away. It is distressing how even the slightest layer of dust spoils running at Craigshire, and (heresy of heresies!) I sometimes wish that I had adopted the stud-contact system of electrification instead of two-rail. Stud-contact at least gives a positive sliding and self-cleaning contact to one motor brush, and the contact made by the wheels of an entire train to the other!

The second recent addition to the Craigshire loco-motive stud is 'Glen Roy'. This is not entirely—or even mainly—my own work, but is an assembled Gem kit bought at a bargain price from my local hobby shop. As bought, it was undetailed and in B.R. black, so I had to add such things as the Westinghouse pump, footplate details and cab glazing, and then re-paint in N.B. colours. I flatter myself that I managed the lining a little bit better than I usually do. Again, this was done the good old-fashioned way with draughtsman's pen and fine sable 'OO' paint brush, using thinned down Humbrol oil paints. I have tried using Letraset-type lining and lettering on models, but find that after I have had the sheets on hand for a year or two they lose a good deal of their tackiness. Even when new they have a horrible habit of half stripping themselves off again when I lift the blue 'rubbing down' paper. I must say that I very much regret the passing of Letraset's original system of letter transfers which made use of a silk screen to transfer the letters which were floated whole and entire off their backings and could be juggled around for quite a while before being finally fixed down. Un-fortunately only a limited range of alphabets were made available for this process before the whole system was changed to the less finicky but also less positive rub-down style of transfer now so common. So, as far as 'Glen Roy' was concerned, it was back to the paintbrush. However, to aid my work I nowadays make use of one of those binocular-vision magnifiers

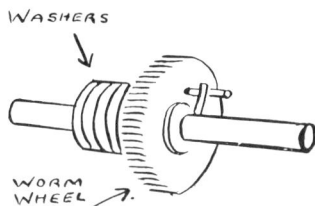

WASHERS

WORM WHEEL

"Morag"—the C.M.R.'s steam-tram type of locomotive leaving Durdreich with the two American style coaches which have given yeoman service for the past twenty-five years, and which have now been thoroughly overhauled and rebuilt to slightly smaller dimensions.

which are advertised from time to time in the model railway press. For someone whose eyesight is not what it was this is an invaluable tool, and I wish I had acquired one years ago.

One of the difficulties in lining is the problem of covering up mistakes and correcting the lines in those places where one's hand has wobbled a bit. There is a limit to the number of times one can cover up a splodge of lining colour with a camouflaging spot of basic body colour or vice versa. However, I have found that so long as one allows the basic body colour several weeks to dry and harden, one can (within limits) remove faulty lining altogether with a quick rub of a turpentine-soaked cloth without damaging the body colour at all—provided this is done within a couple of minutes of the lining being first applied. This does at least give one the opportunity to try again should it become obvious as soon as one has started that things are not going right. In the case of 'Glen Roy's' tender numbers I had to 'rub out' three times before I got things to my satisfaction.

The trackwork on the new layout is a glorious mixture of commercial and home made, mostly salvaged from the previous layout. The standard gauge track is mainly Welkut or A.B.C. chaired track, while the points are mainly Firmway. All these tracks use thin fibre or plastic sleepering which is easier to ballast than the modern thick-sleepered varieties. They also all have wider sleeper spacing which is more suitable for pre-Grouping track than the modern close-spaced style. Actually I did not have enough of the older track to meet my requirements and had to steal track from the hidden storage sidings which were then relaid with new modern track.

The narrow gauge track is largely home-built, although there are stretches of Peco 'crazy' track, and also some of the original Lone Star N gauge track which looked much more like 4mm scale narrow gauge track than the 2mm scale standard gauge track which

"Calum"—one of the C.M.R.'s diminutive 0-4-0s at the Pier Station. This is a free-lance design built on top of one of the ever-useful Arnold Rapido 'N' gauge 0-6-0 chassis with the centre wheels removed.

it was supposed to be. Some of the pointwork makes use of the excellent brass, nickel-plated frogs-cum-wing-rails which Peco marketed for a time shortly after the War. I try to keep the tops of wing rails and check rails painted dull rust colour—as per prototype—but track cleaning operations have a nasty habit of wiping them clean again, as it is only too apparent from the photographs.

I am going to try, on the new layout, to be more punctilious about the use of locomotive lamps than I was on my previous layouts. Most of my 'better' locomotives already have lamp brackets, and they can be added to the other locomotives as the need arises—that is when I can really get down to some proper operation. The lamps I am at present using are the little cast white metal ones as supplied by W. & H. Ltd. and I have rounded the sides of some of these to make them look more like proper N.B.R. or N.E.R. lamps. Proper rounded lamps are now actually available from Pendon. They are fitted with tiny white jewellery 'brilliants' which wink and glow in a most realistic manner as a train progresses around the track and the light catches their many facets. Red brilliants are equally effective when used in tail-lamps.

Mention of these brilliants is illustrative of the hundred and one minor matters with which one can get involved when modelling railways. It never comes to an end. I find that there is always a host of projects in mind clamouring for attention and diverting me from the main task of building the layout. There is, for example, the little matter of Craigshire's bird and animal population. New possibilities here have been opened up by the arrival on the market of the little white metal ducks, swans, seagulls, cats and other fauna produced by MS models. Then there is the challenging problem of producing realistic 4mm scale heather and rose-bay willow-herb, about which I have some bright ideas. There is the signalling to be completed; there are all those kits waiting to be assembled; there are isolating sections to be installed in the hidden storage sidings so that trains can be stopped at the correct places and held there while others are brought into service. As I say, there is no end to it . . . and you sometimes hear people say that they don't know what to do with their spare time or even, because of that, that they 'dread retirement' . . . obviously they aren't railway modellers!

P. D. Hancock

The passenger footbridge at Craig Station. An experimental low-level shot taken with the Exakta camera.

Appendix 1
Operating timetable

No.	Type of Train	Journey	Route	Usual locomotive	Remarks
1.	Through Goods Train	Edinburgh to Craig	Westbound (DOWN)	N.E. 0-8-0	Two circuits. Train arrives at Craig. Loco uncouples, runs to sheds. Yard shunter marshals wagons into sorting sidings.
2.	Local Passenger (Miners' Train).	Craig to Altbeg	Eastbound (UP)	N.B. 0-6-0T	One or two circuits. Can work Altbeg yard if desired.
3.	Express Passenger	Newcastle to Craig	Eastbound (UP)	N.E. 4-4-0	Train appears from storage siding. 2 circuits. Loco uncouples, runs to sheds, and is turned. Train usually of E. Coast Joint Stock 6-wheelers
4.	Passenger Narrow-gauge	Dundreich to Craig	DOWN	"Alistair" or "Ian"	Upon arrival, loco runs to coaling stage.
5.	Possible Special Train.				
6.	Local Goods train	Craig to Altbeg and Dundreich	Westbound (DOWN)	N.B. 0-6-2T or 0-6-0 tender loco	Wagons marshalled at Craig by yard shunter before journey. After arrival back at Craig, loco proceeds to sheds. Yard shunter distributes wagons.
7.	Local Passenger	Altbeg to Craig	Eastbound (UP)	N.B. 0-6-0T	Two circuits. Train enters Craig station bay.

APPENDIX ONE

8.	Passenger Narrow-gauge	Craig to Dundreich	UP	"Angus" or "Roderick"	Loco runs from coaling stage, round train, and pulls train to Dundreich. Uncouples, runs to shed.
9.	East-Coast London to Edinburgh Pullman runs round layout. (At same time as narrow-gauge train above).				
10.	Local Narrow-gauge goods	Dundreich to Craig	DOWN	"Colin" or "Calum"	Train runs into passing loop. Loco shunts siding. Loco runs round and waits on passing loop.
11.	Additional westbound goods train, if necessary.				
12.	Express Passenger	Craig– Altbeg– Edinburgh	Westbound (DOWN)	N.B. 4-4-2T	Continuation of No. 3 above. Train of E. Coast Joint Stock 6-wheelers. 2 circuits. Train runs into Altbeg station and (theoretically) continues to Edinburgh.
13.	Local Passenger	Edinburgh to Craig	Westbound (DOWN)	N.B. 4-4-0 or C.R. 0-4-4T	Train appears from storage sidings. Two circuits. Loco to sheds.
14.	Passenger Narrow-gauge	Craig to Dundreich	UP	Railbus	Train at Dundreich is shunted to run-round loop. Railbus runs into station.
15.	Local passenger	Craig to Berwick	Westbound (DOWN)	N.E. 4-4-0	Loco from sheds on to coaches from train No. 13 above. Two circuits. Train runs into storage sidings.
16.	Local Goods train	Craig to Peter Allan's and Altbeg	Eastbound (UP)	N.E. 0-6-0 tender goods loco	Worked as No. 6 above, in reverse direction.
17.	Local Passenger	Berwick to Craig	Westbound (DOWN)	N.B. 4-4-0 or C.R. 0-4-4T	Train appears from storage siding. Two circuits. Loco to sheds, and turns.
18.	Passenger Narrow-gauge	Dundreich to Craig	DOWN	Railbus	Railbus runs to Craig. Train at Dundreich is run back into station.
19.	Additional eastbound goods train, if necessary.				
20.	Local Passenger	Craig to Edinburgh	Westbound (DOWN)	N.B. 4-4-0 or C.R. 0-4-4T	Loco from sheds on to coaches from train No. 17 above. Two circuits. Train runs into storage siding.
21.	Express Passenger	Edinburgh– Altbeg– Newcastle	Westbound (DOWN)	N.B. 4-4-2T	Train backs out of Altbeg. Two circuits. Loco uncouples at Craig, and runs to sheds.
22.	Passenger Narrow-gauge	Dundreich to Craig	DOWN	"Angus" or "Roderick."	Train runs from Dundreich station platform to Craig. Loco runs to coaling stage
23.	East-Coast London to Edinburgh Pullman runs round layout. (At same time as narrow-gauge train above).				
24.	Local Narrow-gauge goods	Craig to Dundreich	UP	"Colin" or "Calum"	Train runs into station. Loco runs round and backs train into siding (or runs into goods lead and into bridge end siding).

116

Photographs of models taken from ground level can often be very effective because they show them from the height at which we are most accustomed to view the real thing. Unfortunately it has not been easy to take such photographs of Craigshire because most of the photography has been done with a 9 cm × 12 cm plate camera which simply cannot take a photograph from ground level unless it can be positioned immediately in front of the baseboard. The obvious answer would appear to be to use a 35 mm camera, but it is not always easy to fit the camera in the desired position without removing buildings and other pieces of ground-level scenery which get in the way. Here, however, there was no difficulty in placing an Exakta camera on the tracks in front of Altbeg Station, and the result is quite a pleasing shot of N.E.R. 4-4-0 No. 1621 at the head of her train of six-wheelers. (I know the number on the buffer beam is 1630, but this was a mistake on the part of the paint shop!)

25.	Express Passenger	Craig–Altbeg–Newcastle (T.C. to Altbeg)	Eastbound (UP)	N.E. 4-4-0	Two circuits. Train of East Coast Joint Stock 6-wheelers and local Altbeg clerestories, dropped at Altbeg after second circuit. Train then runs into storage siding.
26.	Through Goods train	Craig to Newcastle	Westbound (DOWN)	N.E. 0-8-0	Two circuits. Train runs into storage siding to leave long siding at Craig clear.
27.	Passenger Narrow-gauge	Craig to Dundreich	UP	"Alistair" or "Ian"	Train runs into station. Loco runs round and backs on to train ready to depart next day.
28.	Any extra train required.				
29.	Local Passenger or Mixed	Craig to Altbeg	Westbound (DOWN)	N.B. 0-6-0	4-wheel coaches to Altbeg. (Can also take wagons to Altbeg Yard).
30.	Local Passenger	Altbeg to Craig	Eastbound (UP)	N.B. 0-6-0	4-wheel coaches and clerestories from train No. 25 above. Train runs into main platform. Loco to sheds. Yard shunter distributes coaches.

Appendix 2
Rolling stock

The C.M.R.'s first brake van was obviously inspired by the Tal y Llyn Railway's booking-office on wheels. Like the Company's first coach, it had ordinary "OO" underframes and wheels attached to a false floor.

A couple of the rather large ex-Woolworth's hopper wagons. These were originally painted in bright colours and so were dunked in a caustic soda solution preparatory to re-painting However, the original paintwork was not entirely removed by this, and the wagons emerged from the treatment looking decidedly shabby, with mottled streaks of the original paintwork still adhering in patches to the pitted, almost rusty-looking sides. In short, they looked so marvellously dilapidated that they were left as they were, so that visitors could pass flattering comments upon our skilful "weathering techniques."

The American influence which was at one time so rampant in Craigshire is here revealed in the shape of the C.M.R. work-vehicle—an open wagon and brake van combined. This contained tool boxes, coils of wire and anything and everything else which Angus McPhwat felt might be needed to deal with any likely or unlikely emergency along the right of way.

The C.M.R.'s first passenger coach was a four-wheeler disguised as a bogie coach. No suitable bogie frames or small-size diameter wheels were available, so ordinary 4 mm scale wagon frames and wheels were used. These were attached to a dummy floor which came up to window level, thus enabling the coach sides (Hanson's embossed card G.N.S.R. sides) to come close down to rail level. Even beneath these there were slotted wheelguards concealing the imposture to the best of their ability.

The opportunity to obtain Kemtron photo-engraved coach sides and lost-wax narrow-gauge bogie castings enabled the C.M.R. to build two much more opulent bogie coaches, very reminiscent of those on the Denver and Rio Grande Western. These have handled the bulk of the C.M.R.'s passenger traffic throughout most of its history, and only very recently has a third coach of this type been added to the stock.

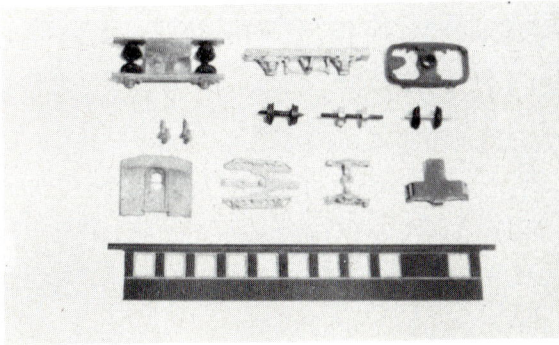

The Kemtron coach and wagon parts laid out and ready for assembly. In the top row there are also a Stewart Reidpath "HO" wagon underframe and a Rokal "TT" bogie frame.

The first goods wagon on the C.M.R. was much larger than I liked due to the difficulty of obtaining suitable narrow-gauge underframes and wheels. In fact, "HO" gauge underframes and expensive, privately-produced wheels were the best I could manage, and the wagon was therefore supposed to be a sort of "maximum dimensions" effort along the lines of the four-wheel wagons on the Vale of Rheidol Railway—virtually scaled-down versions of normal standard-gauge wagons.

Another "maximum dimensions" vehicle was this hopper body mounted on an adapted "OO" coach bogie. This also was fitted with my expensive, privately-produced wheels, but later vehicles were able to make use of wheels for the newly introduced "TT" gauge, or else of Kemtron "HON 3" wheels from the United States.

A much smaller and more satisfactory wagon became possible when the C.M.R. managed to get hold of half a dozen toy wagon bodies marketed by Richard Kohnstam Ltd. These, fitted with Kemtron wheels, had to satisfy us until the advent of Eggerbahn, Playcraft, and other genuine narrow-gauge vehicles.

Bogie vehicles were much easier, and at one time the C.M.R. had five or six of these Rokal "TT" gauge wagon bodies mounted on a variety of bogies—mostly "HON 3" varieties from Kemtron—but also including some home-made efforts. One of these must have had very badly soldered joints, and is for ever memorable because it actually disintegrated while in service, causing a "prototypical" derailment which was almost a pleasure to watch.

A rather special bogie vehicle adapted from an American "HON 3" gauge kit of parts. This actually had fully sprung bogies, the springing being accomplished by means of a couple of little coil springs resting on spigots attached to the bottom of the sideframes and underneath the bogie bolsters.

Another of the C.M.R.'s little work cars, photographed on the rather pleasant stretch of track which used to run alongside the road at Craighill. The vehicle was simply a narrow-gauged motor bogie with the front of a Dinky Toy mechanical horse and other bits and pieces added. The Welsh moss weeds in the foreground look rather dramatic.

More track and roadside detail as seen looking down from the lower slopes of Craighill.

The C.M.R.'s railcar—a Kemtron "Thomas Flyer" used by the Company as a work car and capable of carrying just about everything, including the kitchen sink. There is quite a bit of interesting detail in this photograph, from the trackside weeds to the rather dilapidated loading platform and metal milk churns.

"Agnes" crossing the rather flimsy trestle bridge just outside Ormistone. There is an airiness about this photograph which I rather like. The cellophane water looks more realistic than usual, perhaps because the ripples in it have been accentuated by the broken shadows of the bridge.

Most of the photographs in this book have been taken on Kodak P 1200 or Ilford HP 3 plates with the aid of an old 9 × 12 cm plate camera which I picked up for £5 in the Isle of Man many years ago. I do actually possess a couple of good 35 mm cameras, but for photographing models I still prefer getting my head under a cloth and examining the image I hope to photograph on the ground-glass screen of the plate camera.

My adherence to this camera is, I suppose, a further consequence of my discipleship of John H. Ahern who, in 1946, produced a little booklet on model photography* which still remains my bible for this kind of photographic work. Much of its advice is somewhat dated in these days of precision miniature single lens reflex cameras and electronic flash; but SLRs and electronic flash outfits cost a lot of money, whereas an old plate camera can still be picked up for a few pounds, and ordinary tungsten lights are quite satisfactory for most lighting purposes, provided one has no objection to long time exposures. I myself have taken some photographs of the C.M.R. by available room light, with the lens stopped right down in order to get as much depth of field as possible, and the exposure has taken almost half an hour. I am prepared to admit that this is probably carrying things too far !

* Photographing Models. By John H. Ahern, F.R.P.S. Published by Percival Marshall & Co. Ltd., London. 1946.

Things that might have been

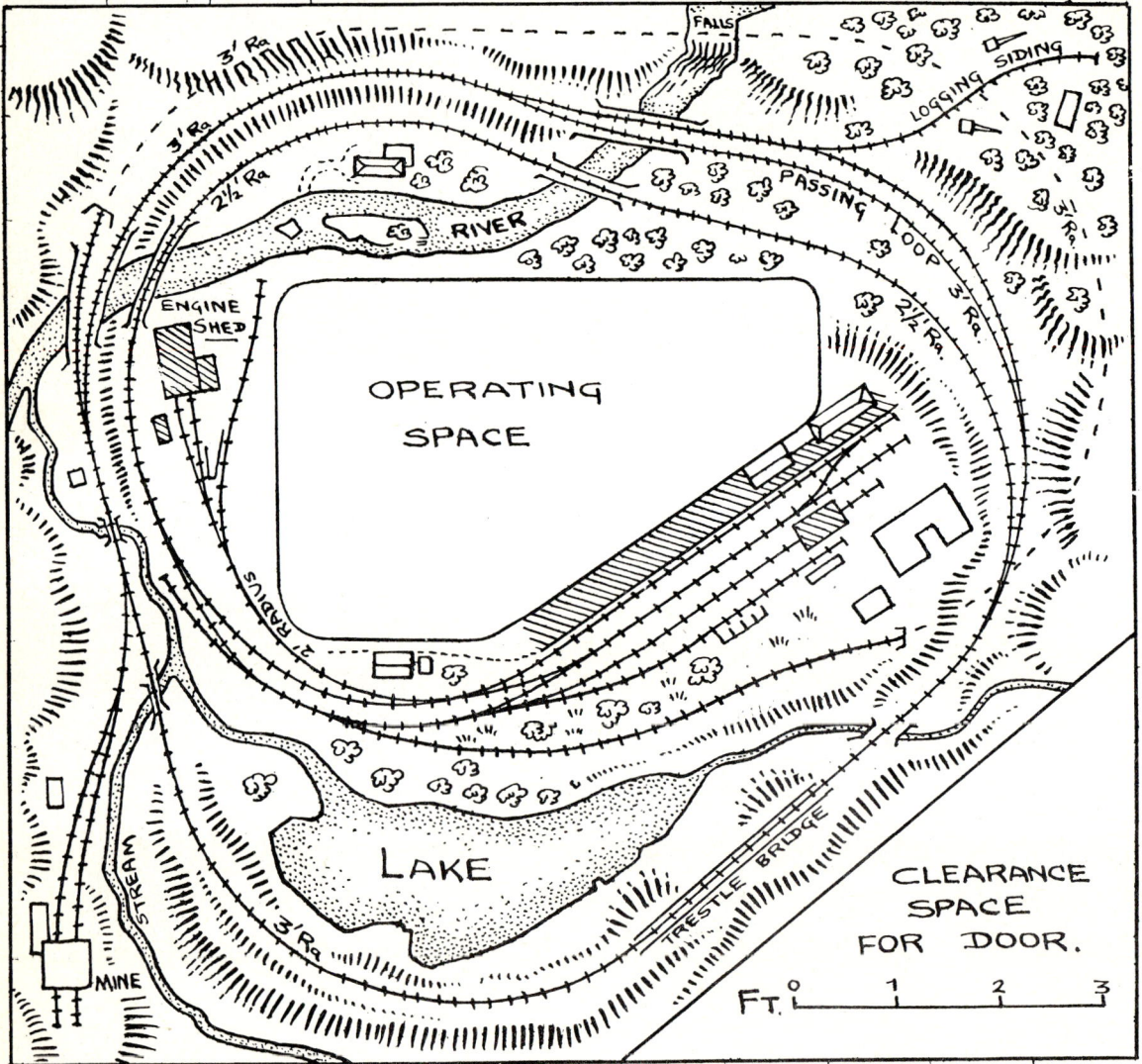

A completely different idea for the C.M.R. was this early
plan, based more upon American than upon British ideas.
The emphasis was to have been upon the scenically
spectacular, but there was plenty of space available for
development, and it was intended eventually to build a
townscape at the back of the station and around the
"logging siding". There were, I think, some quite interesting
possibilities in the plan, but the final result would certainly
have been nothing like the Craigshire with which I am so
familiar today. Anyway, it presupposed the undivided use
of a whole room for the layout, and this never became
available.

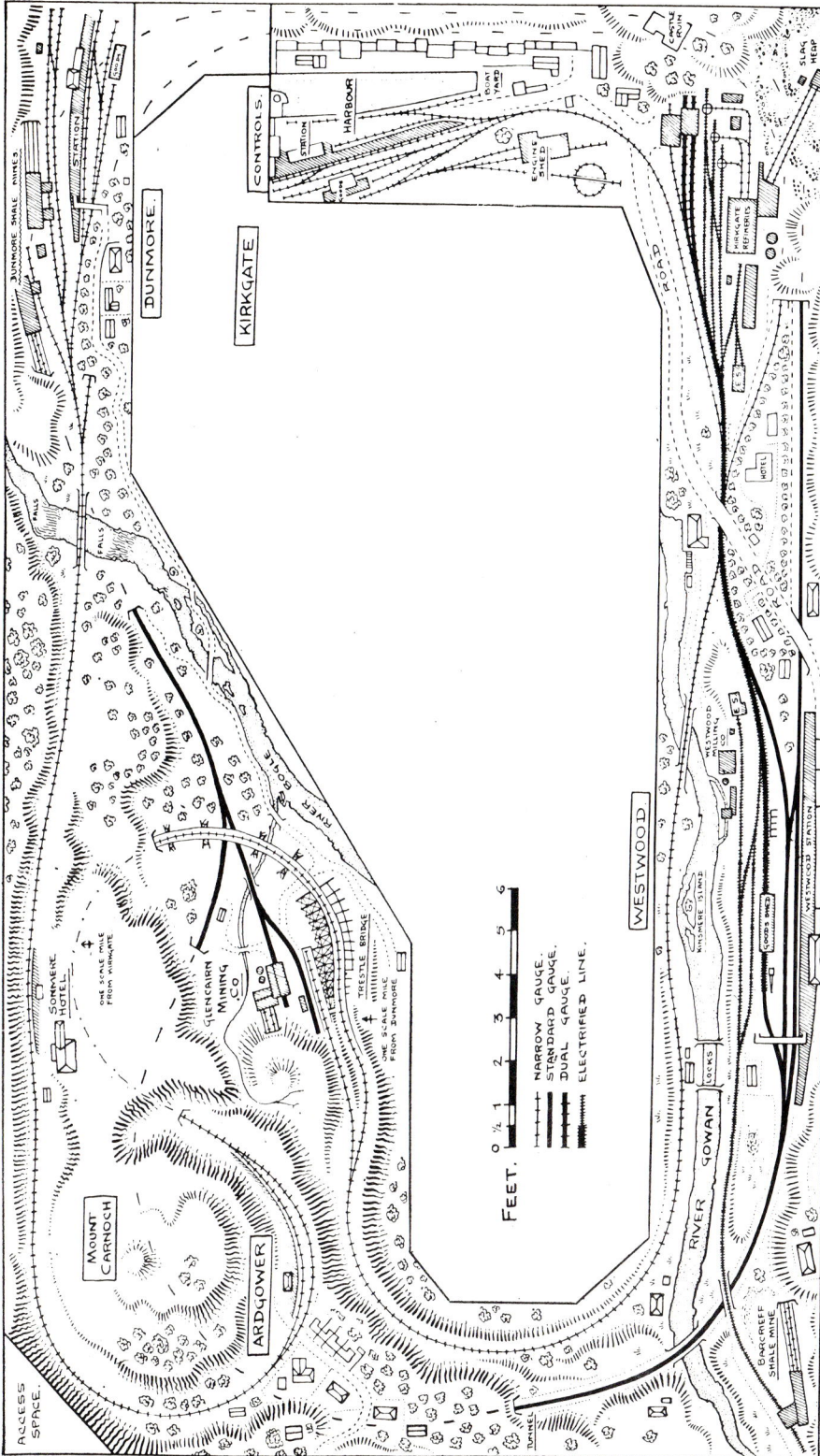

Labels on the plan: JUNMORE SHALE MINES, STATION, DUNMORE., KIRKGATE, CONTROLS, STATION, HARBOUR, BOAT YARD, CASTLE, SLAG HEAP, ENGINE SHED, KIRKGATE SIDINGS, ROAD, FALLS, RIVER GOWAN, SONMORE HOTEL, ONE SCALE MILE FROM KIRKGATE, GLENCAIRN MINING CO., TRESTLE BRIDGE, ONE SCALE MILE FROM DUNMORE, HOTEL, WESTWOOD MINING CO., WESTWOOD, WESTWOOD STATION, KNIMORE ISLAND, FORD'S SHED, MOUNT CARNOCH, ARDGOWER, RIVER GOWAN, LOCKS, BARCREFF SHALE MINE, TUNNEL, ACCESS SPACE.

FEET. 0 ½ 1 2 3 4 5 6

NARROW GAUGE.
STANDARD GAUGE.
DUAL GAUGE.
ELECTRIFIED LINE.

If, on the other hand, an unknown rich uncle had died, leaving me a million pounds (so that I could have devoted myself entirely to worthwhile pursuits and had a little more time for the C.M.R.) then it might have been possible to have gained access to a room about 33 ft by 20 ft (10 by 6 metres)—in which case Craigshire might have developed something like this. Actually, although Craig is quite recognizable here, it has been disguised as "Kirkgate", and the whole plan formed the basis of a mythical dream-layout—the Kirkgate and Dunmore Light Railway—which I described in the January 1954 issue of the American "Railroad Model Craftsman". If I were designing such a large expansion of Craigshire today a great deal would be done differently, but I should not be surprised if the final result were, in fact, to look a little bit like the K. & D.L.R. However, the opportunity to make this anything more than a dream is never likely to arise. (E.R.N.I.E., are you listening?)

RAISED BEADING

CENTRE OF BOGIE BEARING PLATE

CENTRE OF BOGIE BEARING PLATE.

LAMP TOP

ACETYLENE GAS LINE

LAMP FITTINGS

ACETYLENE GENERATOR

BLIND.

LUGGAGE RACK

MIRROR

LAMP BRACKET

BUFFER SHANK

THREADED 10 B.A. TO SCREW INTO BUFFER BEAM

BUFFER HEAD

THE SLOT IN THE BUFFER HEAD IS 2 m.m. WIDE FOR THE COUPLINGS FITTED WITH HOOKS; 3 m.m. WIDE FOR THOSE WITHOUT HOOKS. THE HEAD IS SOLDERED TO THE SHANK.

CENTRAL BUFFER -COUPLING DETAILS (BRASS)

HOOK IS SECURED IN BUFFER SHANK BY A LENGTH OF BRASS WIRE PASSED THROUGH THE HOLES, BENT OVER THE TOP OF THE SHANK TO ACT AS A STOP PREVENTING THE HOOK RISING TOO FAR, AND SOLDERED IN PLACE.

SMALL IRON DISC SOLDERED TO TAIL OF HOOK TO ACT AS MAGNETIC UNCOUPLER.

WIREGAUZE LUGGAGE NET.

BLINDS OF DOWEL ROD

MIRROR OF POLISHED NICKEL-SILVER.

METAL COACH SIDE

CELLULOID SHEET

SCRIBED WOOD PANEL

PAPER DOOR STRAP

RUNNING BOARD

FLOOR

SCRIBED WOOD PARTITION

SUGGESTED COMP-ARTMENT CONSTRUCTION.

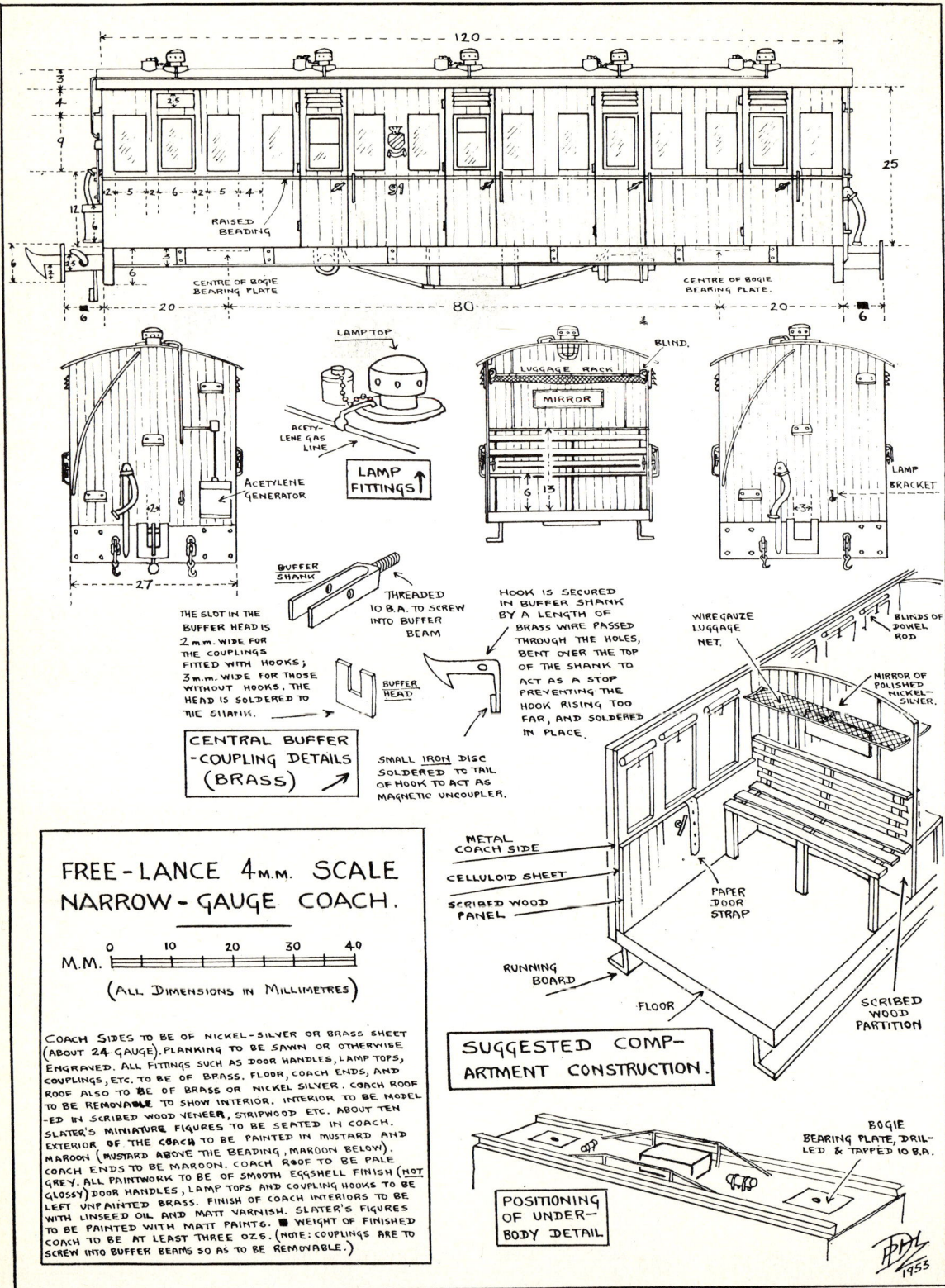

FREE-LANCE 4 M.M. SCALE NARROW-GAUGE COACH.

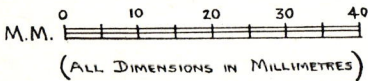

M.M. 0 10 20 30 40

(ALL DIMENSIONS IN MILLIMETRES)

COACH SIDES TO BE OF NICKEL-SILVER OR BRASS SHEET (ABOUT 24 GAUGE). PLANKING TO BE SAWN OR OTHERWISE ENGRAVED. ALL FITTINGS SUCH AS DOOR HANDLES, LAMP TOPS, COUPLINGS, ETC. TO BE OF BRASS. FLOOR, COACH ENDS, AND ROOF ALSO TO BE OF BRASS OR NICKEL SILVER. COACH ROOF TO BE REMOVABLE TO SHOW INTERIOR. INTERIOR TO BE MODEL-ED IN SCRIBED WOOD VENEER, STRIPWOOD ETC. ABOUT TEN SLATER'S MINIATURE FIGURES TO BE SEATED IN COACH. EXTERIOR OF THE COACH TO BE PAINTED IN MUSTARD AND MAROON (MUSTARD ABOVE THE BEADING, MAROON BELOW). COACH ENDS TO BE MAROON. COACH ROOF TO BE PALE GREY. ALL PAINTWORK TO BE OF SMOOTH EGGSHELL FINISH (NOT GLOSSY) DOOR HANDLES, LAMP TOPS AND COUPLING HOOKS TO BE LEFT UNPAINTED BRASS. FINISH OF COACH INTERIORS TO BE WITH LINSEED OIL AND MATT VARNISH. SLATER'S FIGURES TO BE PAINTED WITH MATT PAINTS. ■ WEIGHT OF FINISHED COACH TO BE AT LEAST THREE OZS. (NOTE: COUPLINGS ARE TO SCREW INTO BUFFER BEAMS SO AS TO BE REMOVABLE.)

BOGIE BEARING PLATE, DRILL-ED & TAPPED 10 B.A.

POSITIONING OF UNDER-BODY DETAIL

PDL 1953

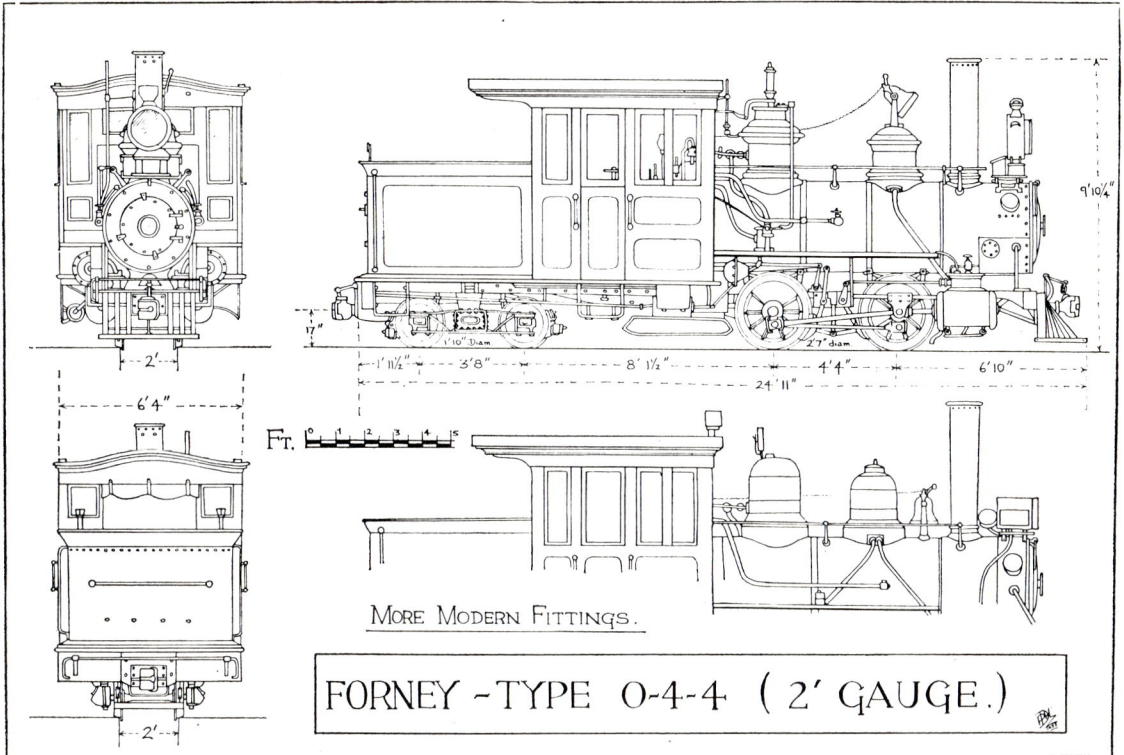

More Modern Fittings.

FORNEY -TYPE 0-4-4 (2' GAUGE.)

I must have been suffering from delusions of grandeur when I drew up plans for these narrow-gauge coaches. The idea was to have three of them, and they were intended to be fitting companions for "Alistair". Alas, this drawing was as far as they ever got—although the three coaches which did emerge (using Kemtron photo-engraved brass sides) were not altogether unworthy of the original high ideals.

Of all the locomotives which were planned for the C.M.R. but never actually built, the one I should most like to see appear at some time in the future would be a model of one of the American Forney-type 0-4-4s which used to run on the Maine 2 ft gauge lines, and some of which are now preserved on the Edaville Railroad at South Carver, Massachusetts. This plan isn't of any one particular locomotive—but was meant to capture the essential essence of the Forneys. One of these days I really will get down to it and build this model.

Index

Kettledrummle passing under the Craig & Mertonford, near Dundreich.

The purpose of this index is to provide quick reference to the principal features of the model, and to indicate where useful information is to be found. No attempt has been made to provide elaborate cross references, or to give each casual mention an entry. The following principles have been used:— Craig, and the Craig & Mertonford Railway have not been individually indexed: the entire book deals with these two items. The other stations on the C.M.R. have been indexed under their initial appearance. Other major features have been indexed on their principal reference. The extensive captions have not been indexed.

The C.M.R. tries to be as self-sufficient as possible and nothing is thrown away that is likely to be of any further use. At least, if it is thrown away it is only thrown as far as the monumental scrap heap at the back of the engine shed—an aerial view of which is here illustrated. The locomotive is "Douglas." She is still more or less intact, but the day will soon come when Angus McPhwat will need a chimney or a dome for another locomotive, and a busy hammering at the back of the sheds will indicate that a new use is being found for some of the temporary scrap there.